Alfred Wills

The Eagle's Nest in the Valley of Sixt

A Summer Home Among the Alps

Alfred Wills

The Eagle's Nest in the Valley of Sixt
A Summer Home Among the Alps

ISBN/EAN: 9783743424043

Manufactured in Europe, USA, Canada, Australia, Japa

Cover: Foto ©Andreas Hilbeck / pixelio.de

Manufactured and distributed by brebook publishing software (www.brebook.com)

Alfred Wills

The Eagle's Nest in the Valley of Sixt

"THE EAGLE'S NEST"

IN THE VALLEY OF SIXT;

A SUMMER HOME AMONG THE ALPS:

TOGETHER WITH SOME

EXCURSIONS AMONG THE GREAT GLACIERS.

BY

ALFRED WILLS,

OF THE MIDDLE TEMPLE, ESQ., BARRISTER-AT-LAW;
AUTHOR OF 'WANDERINGS AMONG THE HIGH ALPS,' AND ONE OF THE
CONTRIBUTORS TO 'PEAKS, PASSES, AND GLACIERS.'

"A wanderer I: I left my much lov'd home,
O'er plain and hill, 'mid ice and snows to roam;
Through many a land my wandering feet have stray'd,
Yet here, at length, content my feet have stay'd."

LONDON
LONGMAN, GREEN, LONGMAN, AND ROBERTS.
1860.

To the Memory
OF
A GENTLE, LOVING, AND MOST ACCOMPLISHED
WIFE,
WHOSE COMPANIONSHIP OR WHOSE SYMPATHY
LIGHTENED EVERY SELF-IMPOSED LABOUR,
AND ENHANCED EVERY PLEASURE
RECORDED HERE,

These Pages,
CONCERNING SCENES AND PLANS WHICH
HOWEVER FASCINATING IN THEMSELVES,
DERIVED THEIR CHIEF INTEREST IN MY EYES
FROM THE HOPE THAT WE SHOULD
OFTEN AGAIN ENJOY THEM TOGETHER,

Are Dedicated,
WITH A TENDER REGRET
WHICH WILL CEASE, I HOPE, ONLY WITH LIFE
AND AN AFFECTION WHICH I KNOW WILL
LAST AS LONG AS ETERNITY ITSELF

A. W.

PREFACE.

In September 1857, when I was in treaty with the good people of Sixt for the purchase of the very lovely spot to which some of the following pages refer, I promised them that if they would accede to my request, and sell me the little plot of communal ground I wished for, I would make some endeavour to render their beautiful valley better known to the travelling world. In private, I have had many opportunities, which I have not neglected, of doing so; but it is high time the promise should be redeemed in a more ample manner. One motive, therefore, for my publishing this Volume is the hope that it may do a service to the valley, by inducing some who might not otherwise have thought of doing so, to turn aside and visit it. I have been especially desirous that the publication should not be longer delayed, because the floods of last winter brought great sorrow and heavy loss upon many of the inhabitants. They wrote to ask me to get up a subscription for them; but the name of Sixt is at present so little familiar to English ears, that I felt it would be useless to attempt anything of the sort, and I replied that instead of asking my countrymen for alms, I would try and persuade some of them to give those who had suffered by the inundations the opportunity of *earning* the relief of which they stand in need.

I am not sorry for the three years' interval between the promise and its execution. The beauty of the valley seemed to me so remarkable, that I distrusted at first my own impressions and recollections, and it was not without a lurking anticipation of disappointment, that I returned thither in 1858, accompanied, this time, by my wife, to whom I had frequently expressed, in no measured terms, my estimate of the scenery she was about to see. When, however, I remember that her highly raised expectations were surpassed by the reality; that day by day we discovered new and increasing charms in the neighbourhood; that ever since, the Valley of Sixt has held its place in our memories, after dispassionate retrospect, as the most attractive of the many scenes of beauty we have visited, I can no longer entertain the fear that the natural interest attaching to a hobby has created in my mind impressions which will not be ratified by the soberer judgment of others.

The illustrations are all but one from my wife's sketches, aided now and then by photographs of my own. They are, I believe, quite faithful, though they want the last touches of her ready pencil, the last corrections of her tenacious memory. This volume is, alas! *in memoriam.* It was planned out last year, and a small portion executed, by us both, as a joint production, and this spring we were thinking seriously of proceeding further with it, when this project was put an end to by one of those mysterious dispensations of Providence which try the courage of the stoutest heart. I had been hastily summoned into the country by the unexpected death of my father, and, on my return to London, after the last rites had been paid to him, I was met by the startling intelligence that my wife also was no more. A disease so secret, so insidious, that its very existence had escaped the anxious affection of friends, and eluded the experienced vigilance of a most accomplished medical man, had silently reached its climax, and suddenly arrested the mysterious current of life; and without time for one farewell, the gentlest and most graceful spirit that ever was the light and the pride of a happy home, had passed from earth.

This little work has had, therefore, a peculiar and mournful interest to me. I should be glad indeed, if I could think that its perusal might ever with another, as its preparation has done with myself, make an hour of sorrow flit more lightly by. If it should not do that, it may yet perhaps be the means of inducing some reader or another to visit scenes, the memory of which may one day help him to bear cheerfully and gently the trials of life. These pages will not have been written in vain, if he should then be able to say, with one who knew Nature well, and whose pure and noble spirit turned that knowledge to the best account:—

> " These beauteous forms
> Through a long absence have not been to me
> As is a landscape to a blind man's eye :
> But oft in lonely rooms, and 'mid the din
> Of towns and cities, I have owed to them,
> In hours of weariness, sensations sweet,
> Felt in the blood, and felt along the heart ;
> And passing even into my purer mind
> With tranquil restoration ; feelings too
> Of unremembered pleasure. . . . .
> . . . . Nor less, I trust,
> To them I may have owed another gift
> Of aspect more sublime ; that blessed mood,
> In which the burthen and the mystery,
> In which the heavy and the weary weight
> Of all this unintelligible world
> Is lightened." *

ESHER : *July* 20*th*, 1860.

---

* Wordsworth.

NOTE.

The little sketch-map, intended to show the position of the Valley of Sixt, relatively to the neighbouring districts, is reduced from the Sardinian Government map; the more detailed map of the immediate neighbourhood of Sixt is slightly enlarged from the same original. The Government map is executed in a most elaborate style, but I must say that I am quite unable to reconcile a great deal of it with my own personal knowledge of the district. The characterestic form of the ridge of the Fer à Cheval, for instance, is absolutely wanting; the Pointe de Salles is kept much too far back from the Giffre, and that part of the track to the Col d'Anterne which lies beneath its highest precipices, seems to me quite incorrectly given. These are but instances: one speaks, of course, with a certain degree of hesitation, when backing one's own recollections and impressions against a work authenticated by the stamp of the Royal Staff Corps of Sardinia; but I am unable to help the opinion I have formed, which is, that for all matters of nicety and accurate detail, it is, as to this part at least, utterly unreliable. The very remarkable mountain called the Pic de Tinneverges is not even named in it, and Balmat has several times remarked to me upon the want of exactness of which I complain. Still I have not ventured to alter it on the authority of my memory alone, and indeed a severe attack of illness, which confined me to my bed at the time when it was necessary for the engraver to begin his work, would have made it difficult for me to do so had I wished it. All that I can do, therefore, is to warn the reader against trusting to it, and to say, that if any of my descriptions should be at variance with its representations, I do not admit the map as a conclusive authority against me. A great number of the less important names in the original have been purposely omitted, as they would have served only to produce confusion.

CONTENTS.

CHAPTER I.

THE VALLEY OF THE GIFFRE, FROM TANNINGES TO SIXT.

Situation of Sixt.—The Road from Bonneville.—First Sight of the Valley.—Its Richness.—Samoëns.—The "Croix d'Or."—Excursions in the Neighbourhood.—The Road to Sixt.—Gorge of Les Tines.—Pointe de Salles.—Sixt.—The Hotel.—Marie.—La "Cuisine Moccand" . . . . Page 1

CHAP. II.

THE FER À CHEVAL, THE FOND DE LA COMBE, AND THE FATE OF JACQUES BALMAT.

The Pic de Tinneverges.—The Fer à Cheval.—The Fond de la Combe.—A Tragical Incident.—Disappearance of Jacques Balmat.—A Revelation.—The Hunter taken off his Guard.—Motives of the Syndic.—The Chalets of Boret.—Caterpillars' Paradise.—Landslips of the Tête Noire.—The Vaudru 30

CHAP. III.

THE LAC DE GERS.

Situation of the Lake.—Beautiful Ascent.—Moccand kept in order.—Exquisite Wood Walk.—View from the Giétà.—Neglect of

Wild Fruits among the Alps.—A dreary Scene.—The Lake—The Montagne de Gers.—A Picture for the Stereoscope.—The Descent.—Remarks . . . . Page 52

CHAP. IV.

THE VALLÉE DES FONDS AND THE "EAGLE'S NEST."

Course of the Haut Giffre.—Salvagny.—The Pointe de Salles.—"Le Rouget" and "La Pleureuse."—Luxuriant Vegetation.—La Croix d'Espérit.—Curious Stratification.—Falls of "Les Joubas."—The Path of the Avalanche.—Precipices of the Buet.—Les Fonds.—Magnificent View from the Plateau.—Love at first Sight.—Management of Communal Affairs.—Proposal to Purchase.—Opposition of the Curé.—Position of the Priests in Sardinia.—Difficulties started.—The Opposition Party the stronger.—Count d'Elia.—A second Deliberation and a casting Vote.—The Count insulted.—Memorials and Counter-memorials.—The Royal Assent obtained.—Monsieur de Bergoëns.—Our Visit in 1858.—Deputations.—A Serenade.—Salutes fired.—Hospitalities.—Generous Behaviour of all Parties.—The "Eagle's Nest" named.—The Chalet planned.—Our Neighbours and their Cordiality 72

CHAP. V.

THE BUET.

Ascent from Chamouni.—The Cascade Bérard.—The "Pierre Bérard."—Rough Quarters.—An unexpected Meeting.—How we passed the Night and how the Guides passed the Night.—Deep Striæ.—Daybreak on Mont Blanc.—The Summit.—Sea of Clouds.—Descent to Sixt.—A wonderful Amphitheatre.—The Chamois.—First Impressions of the Plateau des Fonds.—Ascent from Sixt.—View from the Col de l'Échaud.—Severe Attack of Illness.—A Dilemma.—Forward!—The distant Cattle-bells.—Deep Snow.—The Chalet Bérard reached.—A close Bargain.—A simple Cure 124

CHAP. VI.

THE APPROACHES TO SIXT.

Carriage Roads from Bonneville, Geneva, and Cluses. — The Col d'Anterne, from Servoz to Sixt. — Passage across the Bréven to Chamouni.— From the Plateau d'Anterne to Les Fonds, by the Chemin des Grasses Chèvres.— The Col de l'Échaud.— From the Valley of the Rhone to Samoëns, by the Cols de Coux and De Golèze.— Beauty of Champéry.— The Col de Sagéroux.— Passages to St. Maurice and Martigny . . . . . Page 162

CHAP. VII.

THE FOSSILS OF MOËD.

From Servoz to Moëd. — Les Éboulements. — The Val Dioza.— Moëd. — The Fossil Bed. — A Storm on the Mountains. — A narrow Escape.— An Incident of the Storm on the Mer de Glace. — Second Visit to Moëd. — From Cluses to Sixt.— Les Fonds in the Morning.— Chemin des Grasses Chèvres.— Fossil Teeth.— Rendezvous at Moëd.— Interior of a Chalet.— How we passed the Night.— Sunrise.— Our Cook. — A second Night in the Chalet.— Description of the Fossils.— Springing a Mine.— Descent to the Dioza.— Ascent of the Bréven.— A cool Path.— A Toilette on the Snow.— Chamouni 177

CHAP. VIII.

BAD WEATHER ON MONT BLANC.

Possible Dangers of bad Weather.— Balmat's proposed Experiment. — Dr. Tyndall's Assistance.— Opposition of the chief Guide.— Appeal to the Intendant. — Gorgeous Sunset at the Grands Mulets.— The Corridor.— The Mist comes on.— Summit of Mont Blanc.— Burying the Thermometer.— Intense Cold.— Appearance of our Party.— Balmat's Hands frost-bitten.— His Sufferings.—

Descent of the Mur. — Consideration of the Porters. — Sudden Change of Weather. — State of Balmat's Hands. — Fate of the Thermometer . . . . Page 221

CHAP. IX.
THE COL D'ERIN.

The Glacier du Tour. — Sion. — Val d'Erin. — Curious Pyramidal Formations. — Evolena. — Unpromising Prospects. — A Walk in the Dark. — Glacier de Ferpêcle. — Advance of the Glacier. — Dirt Bands. — Chalets d'Abricolla. — Dangerous Passage. — The Motta Rotta. — The Col. — Striking View of the Matterhorn. — Measurements of Height. — Passing a Bergschrund. — The Stöckhi. — Glacier of Zmutt. — Remarkable Sounds. — Beautiful Descent to Zermatt 247

CHAP. X.
ASCENT OF MONTE ROSA.

Supposed Inaccessibility. — The Schlagintweits. — Messrs. Smyth. — Topography of Monte Rosa. — An old Friend. — Coffee and Quarrels. — A sadder and a wiser Man. — The Comet. — The Gornergrat. — The Gorner Glacier. — Appearance of Monte Rosa. — Ascent of the "Saddle." — Our first Halt. — A terrible Wind. — A narrow Ridge. — The Höchste Spitze. — Grand Panorama. — The Nord End Spitze. — Height of the "Saddle." — Magnificent Crevasses. — Fatiguing Descent. — A pleasant Meeting. — The Riffelberg 258

DIRECTIONS TO THE BINDER.

Maps.

Sketch Map . . . . *to face page*	1
Map of the Valley of Sixt	218

Lithographs.

View of the Plateau des Fonds and the Eagle's Nest . *Frontispiece.*	
Cascade of the "Nant Dant" . . . *to face page*	13
The Pic de Tinneverges	24
The Fer à Cheval	32
Sixt and the Giéta	55
The Pointe de Salles	82
View from the Eagle's Nest, looking towards the Buet .	93
View from the Eagle's Nest, looking down the Valley .	119
The Aiguilles Rouges	126
From the Bridge above the Cascade Bérard . . .	157
View from Champéry	172
Monte Rosa	303

THE NEW
PUBLIC LIB

ASTOR, LEN

"THE EAGLE'S NEST"

ETC.

CHAPTER I.

> " Among steep hills, in woods embosomed, flows
> A copious stream, with boldly winding course,
> Here traceable, there hidden, there again
> To sight restored, and glittering in the sun.
> On the stream's bank and everywhere appeared
> Fair dwellings, single or in social knots,
> Some scattered o'er the level, others perched
> On the hill sides, a cheerful quiet scene."
>
> WORDSWORTH.

> " All that creation's varying mass assumes
> Of grand and lovely here aspires and blooms;
> Bold rise the mountains, rich the gardens glow."
>
> MOORE.

THE VALLEY OF THE GIFFRE, FROM TANNINGES TO SIXT.

SITUATION OF SIXT.—THE ROAD FROM BONNEVILLE.—FIRST SIGHT OF THE VALLEY.—ITS RICHNESS.—SAMOËNS.—THE "CROIX D'OR."— EXCURSIONS IN THE NEIGHBOURHOOD.—THE ROAD TO SIXT.—GORGE OF LES TINES.—POINTE DE SALLES.—SIXT.—THE HÔTEL.—MARIE.— LA "CUISINE MOCCAND."

THE valley of Sixt has been so little visited, that to very many persons who have travelled amongst the Alps, its very name and situation are unknown. Yet from Geneva it is easier of access than the valley of Chamouni; it may be reached in one day from Chamouni or from the valley of the Rhone, and its attractions are second to those of no Alpine valley I have seen. I had always heard it spoken of as a place where there were a great many waterfalls, — a sort of faint praise which seemed to imply that there was not much else to recommend it. It was therefore with something of the pleasant surprise of a new discovery, that when chance took me into the valley, I found it so beautiful that thenceforward I hardly knew how to keep away from it. I first went to Sixt in August 1857, and I returned thither twice that year. In 1858 I went abroad again, accompanied by my wife, who had not been with me the previous year. She was no less delighted than I had been with the scenery, and we spent nearly three weeks there during the autumn. We paid two visits to the valley, the one before, and the other after, a month's ramble amongst the greatest and grandest scenery of Savoy and Switzerland; but the attractions of Sixt remained paramount in our minds, even amidst the exciting scenery of the great glacier world. There is a large class of travellers who, I dare say, would hardly be able to understand this preference, as the number of definite and recognised excursions in the neighbourhood of Sixt is limited; but it was our delight to make ourselves thoroughly acquainted with every nook and corner — to spend day after day quietly loitering about, now in one part of the valley, now of another, sketching, photographing, and botanising — to wander hither and thither as fancy dictated, and not to think that a certain number of miles must be accomplished every day; and we left the valley with the feeling that we did not half know it yet, and that there was plenty of unexplored ground left for future summers.

The little village of Sixt, from which the valley takes its name, lies at the base of the northern spurs of the Buet. It is nearly due north of Chamouni, and across two ranges of mountains, the Bréven and the next chain behind the Bréven, the Chaîne des Fys, a mountain chain of great wildness and rugged grandeur, of which the extreme point to the west is familiar to every traveller to the valley of Chamouni as the Aiguille de Varens, the precipitous peak towering just above St. Martin. Sixt may be approached from Chamouni by a straight cut over these intervening ridges, practicable only for pedestrians, or by a mule-path which leaves the high road half-way between Chamouni and Sallenches. From Geneva there is an excellent carriage-road, passing through Bonneville, where it diverges from the road to Chamouni. The Chamouni road crosses the River Arve, the road to Sixt keeps along its right bank. Every one who has been from Bonneville to Cluses, will remember that between those two places the Arve flows in a valley often several miles wide, inclosed between two parallel ranges of mountains; those on the right of the traveller to Chamouni being steep and lofty, those on the opposite or eastern side of the valley being lower, more cultivated, and in many parts luxuriantly wooded. The valley of Sixt lies behind this eastern boundary of the valley of the Arve, and the road from Bonneville to Sixt crosses the range nearly opposite to Cluses. There is a second carriage-route from Geneva to Sixt, which quits the Bonneville road at Annemasse, and forking off to the left passes behind the range of mountains which lie to the left of the traveller on his way from Annemasse to Bonneville, and culminate in the conical summit of the Môle, just above Bonneville. It is considerably shorter than the road through Bonneville, but at present it is not in a good state. When I was last at Sixt, a project was on foot for putting it in order: if that be ever done, the time of transit from Geneva to Sixt will be abridged by some two hours, and Sixt will be brought within little more than half a day's journey from Geneva. At present, by way of Bonneville, with a carriage and pair, about ten or twelve hours are needed for the journey. It is not so far as from Geneva to Chamouni, but the diligence service is very slowly and indifferently performed, and of course a carriage with one pair of horses cannot travel with anything like the speed of a diligence, which has successive relays to depend upon. I shall now ask the reader to start with me from Bonneville, and accompany me along the road by the eastern or right bank of the Arve.

About five miles above Bonneville, the Giffre, the stream which belongs to the valley of Sixt, effects its junction with the Arve; in its own proper valley it flows nearly parallel with this part of the Arve; but having found a convenient gap in the mountain range that has long formed its boundary, just at the eastern base of the Môle, it has seized the opportunity, turned sharply to the left, and escaped through the unguarded opening, to swell the flood of the Arve. The road leaves the point of junction to the right, and traversing the flat ground at the base of the Môle, crosses the Giffre a mile or two above the junction of the two streams at a little village called

Marignier. It then hugs the base of the hills which form the eastern boundary of the valley of the Arve, and makes for the spot where they are most easily crossed, a depression in the range nearly opposite the village of Cluses, on the Chamouni road. There is here a long and steep ascent, up which it is often pleasant to walk; for the road is well shaded, passing between rows of fruit-trees which overhang the road, and amongst fertile fields sprinkled with chalets. The view across the valley is most striking, as you look up the splendid ravine towards Sallenches, with the village of Cluses sparkling at its entrance, and some of the snowy spurs of Mont Blanc towering above in the distance.

At length you fairly turn your back upon Cluses and the Chamouni road, and after winding by two or three shady zigzags past the picturesque old castle of Chatillon, the road is carried for a few hundred yards over the table land forming the lowest point in the ridge. Presently you come to a row of sturdy, weather-beaten beeches, casting a deep and refreshing shade upon the road, and find yourself at the entrance of what seems like another world. A wide and fertile valley lies almost beneath your feet, shut in on each side by mountain ranges which, anywhere but among the Alps, would be called lofty.

They present an exquisite combination of grandeur and of softer beauty. Clothed to a great height with woods, in which the dark foliage of fir and pine is pleasantly relieved by the brighter green of the beech, they afford conclusive evidence that the severities of an Alpine climate do not visit even their highest portions; but they often break away into abrupt faces of rock, of no inconsiderable height, or are crowned by rugged peaks of a bold and precipitous character. Bright slopes of lawn-like pasture mingle with the darker green of the forest trees, and dispute with them the possession of the mountain sides. Numerous chalets, of a better order than usual, nestle beneath the shelter of the woods, or are dotted about the upland meadows. In the centre of the valley the Giffre pours down its discoloured stream, the drainage of the glaciers of the Buet and of the Pic de Tinneverges. At no great distance from where you stand, the prosperous little town of Tanninges sparkles in the sunlight, and nearer still stands a great block of dingy building by the river side, surrounded by an immense walled garden, formerly the Jesuits' College.

The plain through which the Giffre threads its way is still more rich and verdant than the mountain chains that bound it; it is thickly studded with orchards and corn-fields, and is characterised by a general appearance of uncommon comfort and prosperity. At the head of this beautiful valley, the eye and the mind are alike arrested by the great crags and extended snows of the Buet, which seem to say that in this direction at least nature has done her best, by denying the means of egress, to complete the resemblance of the scene to the "Happy Valley."

The road winds down from the top of the hill by several zigzags. The traveller on foot will probably take a short cut or two across the swampy hedgeless fields, and thus arrive more quickly at the foot of the descent, where a stone bridge spans the dirty waters of the Giffre. If he knows his way, he will now desert the road which leads across the little plain to the village of Tanninges, and turning sharply to the right, between a little inn and the river, will follow a footpath running beside the long and lofty wall of the convent garden, and emerging on to the green fields half a mile or more beyond the village. A mile at the very least is gained by this short cut. On reaching the end of the convent garden wall, you can either turn to the left and rejoin the road at once, or if the weather be dry, you can keep to the fields for some time longer. There is no fear of doing any damage in the autumn. The hay crop has been got in, and the inhabitants of the valley are pleasant and obliging to strangers. The only attack likely to be made is from one of the numerous and ill-conditioned curs that abound here, as throughout Switzerland and Sardinia, to whom a liberal allowance of alpen-stock would be of no small service.

The road is now thickly lined with apple, pear, and walnut-trees, which yield a welcome shade from the noonday sun. The valley is hot, as the richness of the flora, the greenness of the hills on either hand, the vigorous growth of trees and fruits, and the abundance of butterflies and lizards attest. The mountain ranges which flank the valley present scenes of rare pastoral beauty. Fertile upland farms, dotted with substantial homesteads, and guarded by vast variegated woods, not of fir and pine, but of all sorts of forest trees, as varied as those which clothe the beautiful steeps of Norbury Park, or deck the princely slopes of Chevening, rise just above the plain, and are crowned by broad tracts of the richest mountain pasture land, vying in depth of green with the most favoured spots in the Simmenthal, or the still richer valley of Champéry. As you ascend the valley, the mountains close in on either hand, the trees are finer still, the forests more extensive, the grass greener, the signs of rustic wealth and prosperity greater. There is but one dull stretch of road—where a straggling pine wood, covering an extensive swamp, interferes with the enjoyment of the prospect, and here the barberry grows in profusion by the road side, and the eye is distracted from the monotony of the pine wood by the singular beauty of the delicate clusters of bright scarlet berries.

Some two or three hours after leaving Tanninges, the scenery, while preserving the same general character as that already described, attains perhaps its greatest beauty. The spurs of the mountain chain on the left advance their wooded bases somewhat into the plain. Mingled with the leafy glories of the ancient forests are broad patches of well-cultivated land, or trim and closely shaven meadow slopes, looking at a little distance like English lawns, and ornamented with picturesque chalets or substantial farm buildings. One conspicuous knoll is crowned by the tapering spire of a time-honoured chapel. At the foot of this knoll lies the thriving little town of Samoëns, a large straggling assemblage of well-built houses, in the midst of a rich tract of orchards, pasture grounds, and farm lands, stretching for half a mile or a little more from the town to the river, which runs just beneath the base of the mountain range on the right,—a range, perhaps, still richer and more productive than its opposite eastern rival, and giving birth, at a short distance from the village, to a foaming waterfall of no common gracefulness and beauty. On every hand are the signs of wealth and comfort. No squalid buildings meet the eye, no stunted forms whose cowering aspect speaks of want and misery. The men are a fine, broad-shouldered race; the women strong and healthy, and though in middle life tanned and disfigured by field-work, are, when young, particularly comely and pleasing both in face and manners. The children are for the most part hearty and well clad, and their parents would be ashamed to permit them to indulge in the mendicancy and extortion so familiar to the traveller on the road to Chamouni. The village boasts a "place," or little square, one side of which is occupied by the church, and in the middle of which grows a magnificent and patriarchal linden-tree—the Palladium of Samoëns, as the judge of the district informed me—an object of singular affection and respect to the inhabitants. When they quit the village for any length of time, or return to it after any considerable absence, they salute the tree, and when any of them emigrate or travel into distant parts, it rarely happens that they do not carry with them a few of its leaves, which are religiously and affectionately preserved as mementos of the dear old country.

Let me not omit to mention one important feature of Samoëns. It possesses a homely but comfortable hotel, kept by worthy and honest people. The "Croix d'Or" is an excellent specimen of an unsophisticated country inn, and the landlord, M. Pellet, is an intelligent, kind, and attentive host. They can make up from fifteen to twenty beds, and when I last was there, were preparing to increase the accommodation. There is no style or luxury about the place. The landlord and his family perform nearly all the service of the establishment, but the beds are scrupulously clean, the fare is abundant though plain, the cookery simple and wholesome, and the charges moderate. The situation of the hotel is very pleasing, some of the windows looking up a fine opening in the eastern chain, guarded by magnificent cliffs of naked rock, by which a beautiful passage leads to Champéry and the valley of the Rhone; others commanding most attractive views of the little plain of the Giffre, of the green slopes, wooded hills, and comfortable cha-

CASCADE OF THE RANG...

lets on the opposite side of the stream, of the noble cascade of the Nant Dant, and of the fine group of the Buet and his subsidiary mountains at the head of the valley. A balcony, running round two sides of the house, in which I have often taken my tea, is an excellent place from which to watch the glories flung by the setting sun over this charming scene.

Samoëns is a place where I have always regretted my inability to spend one or two days at least, and devote them to exploring the neighbourhood. The few short walks I have had the opportunity of taking on both sides of the valley have given me a very high impression of the beauty of the district, which is better known to the Genevese than to our countrymen, for I was told that several of the pretty chalets I observed crowning some of the most picturesque eminences were little country houses belonging to Genevese gentlemen.

Nearly opposite to Samoëns is a covered bridge over the Giffre. It is approached through a deep fir-wood, carpeted with the richest undergrowth of moss. Crossing the bridge and turning to the left up the course of the stream, you pass beneath a most noble grove of pine-trees. The path, rising and falling gently, leads beyond the fir wood and through open fields, across a soft green sward, and again enters a fine wood, principally of beech and fir. The increasing thunder of a body of water falling from a great height warns you that you are not far from the cascade you saw from the inn; but it scarcely prepares you for the magnificent fall you behold when a few minutes' climb brings you to the skirts of the wood, and shows you the stream pouring over a ledge some seven or eight hundred feet above you, and bounding with one leap into a rocky basin at the foot of the precipice. The roar and spray of the water, the secluded character of the spot, the abruptness of the cliffs on every hand, the richness of the woods that cling to every ledge on which a patch of mould can rest, can hardly fail to produce a deep impression on the most careless spectator. To behold the scene as my wife and I did in the autumn of 1858, by the ruddy glow of a gorgeous sunset, when every object on the opposite side of the valley on which the sunbeams fell was flooded with crimson light, and all nature seemed on fire except the dank, secluded hollow where we stood, is a chance which must fall to the lot of comparatively few. Well might our companion, M. Bergoëns, the excellent and accomplished Intendant of the district, be proud of his native valley, as he pointed out to us its beauties under circumstances which so much enhanced the attractions of even the valley of Sixt.

An equally beautiful walk, starting likewise from the bridge and following for a while the same path, leads up the mountain side, through belts of magnificent trees and across well-kept strips of grass land, to the top of the cascade. Here, as lower down the valley, one cannot fail to be struck with the variety of trees in the wood. Indeed, this is the great characteristic of this district. Generally amongst the Alps there is such a predominance of the fir tribe, that one often thinks of an Alpine wood as a synonym for a pine forest, but throughout this district it is far otherwise. The beech, the birch, the elm, the walnut, the ash, freely mingle their foliage with the darker green of the fir, or the fresh emerald of the larch. In this particular spot the fine growth of the trees is as remarkable as the picturesque and varied aspect of the wood. When I passed through it I was accompanied by my friend Auguste Bulmat, who, like myself, visited it for the first time, and he told me then he thought he had seen nothing like it among the Alps; every stem was so tall and straight, and well-grown on every side. I remember particularly his admiration of the young fir-trees, which he thought would make alpen-stocks of matchless quality. Above the top of the fall we came upon orchards, and upon arable and pasture land of excellent quality and great extent. There was an ample stock of fruit-trees laden with autumnal produce; cows and goats were feeding about, and all the signs of agricultural industry displayed. We got glimpses of pastoral valleys leading high up towards the mountain tops, and offering scenes of great beauty, which it would be well worth while thoroughly to explore. The quantities of wild fruits, strawberries, raspberries, blackberries, and bilberries, that were growing on the mountain side were astonishing. We could pick them at every step; and M. Pellet's son, who was with us, bought a large basketful, containing two or three quarts of fruit, some of which embellished the array of my evening meal, for four sous. He made no secret of the price, and I found no notice of the addition to my tea in the bill. Elsewhere, I should never have heard what was paid for them, but I should certainly have found out that they were not to be had for nothing at an inn. The view from this point is very attractive indeed, embracing nearly the whole extent of the valley from a little below Sixt, past Samoëns, and down to far below Tanninges. Immediately opposite is the fine opening towards the Col de Golèze, partaking of the same character of rich pastoral beauty. The mountain which flanks it on the right is of remarkable aspect. Its outline rises in a graceful sweep, like a surging wave, to its highest point, where it ends abruptly in a vast precipice of many thousand feet, towering in rugged majesty above the commencement of the pass. The woods, chiefly of dark fir, reach to a great height along its side, and are crowned by pasturage somewhat scantier than is usual here. It is said that this upper portion abounds in fossil animal remains, chiefly of belemnites and ammonites, but I have not yet been able to explore it for myself.

The earlier part of the passage of the Golèze forms a pleasant stroll from Samoëns. The morning after I had visited the foot of the cascade of the Nant Dant, I walked up it for two or three miles before the sun was well risen, and while the heavy dew of a clear August morning lay upon the ground, and transformed every blade of grass into a row of sparkling brilliants. When I was obliged reluctantly to turn back, I was more than ever struck with the beauty of the opposite side of the valley, of which I saw now small portions only displayed amidst a foreground of rocks and trees. The knoll on which the little chapel stands, is also a very fine point of view; and, in fact, it is hardly possible to go wrong in any direction from Samoëns.

Perhaps, however, the most interesting walk or

drive of all is that along the main road, leading to Sixt. The scenery becomes still finer as you ascend the valley. The mountain ranges approach nearer to the stream, and are more precipitous and craggy than they were. The road, which has long left the river nearly half a mile on the right, is now forced close to it, and at length the impetuous torrent is rushing wildly by, within a few feet of the road. At this point,—about half an hour's drive above Samoëns,—a remarkable interruption occurs to the generally uniform slope of the valley, which has been gently, if not imperceptibly, rising all the way from Tanninges. A great hill of dark slaty rock rises abruptly to a height of several hundred feet, blocking up the whole of the valley. There is but little mould upon most of the rocky surface—only enough to support a scanty growth of underwood—and the stream is lost in a narrow cleft, not many yards wide, and, perhaps, a hundred and fifty feet deep. A little "station"—as the diminutive wayside shrines are called—decorated with a tawdry image of the Virgin, and held in great esteem by the neighbourhood, marks the highest spot attained by the road, which ascends by steep and ill-made zigzags. Here a few beeches on the right fairly overhang the river, and by clinging to their trunks you may drop a stone, which will fall through a sombre, sunless chasm, damp with the spray of the fretting stream, and will not reach the surface of the water till after an interval of several seconds. The rock is curiously worn and rounded, as if by the action of water; and a little plain beyond has the appearance of an alluvial deposit. The opposite side of the dark rift through which the torrent chafes on its wilful way, is perfectly smooth and polished, and it would seem as if the stream had gradually cut its way down through the opposing barrier, till it had sunk to its present level. If this be really so, a great lake must once have existed behind the rocky eminence, the level of which must have gradually sunk in the course of ages, till it finally disappeared, and left the rich plain below Sixt in its place. This deep waterworn channel of the torrent affords no bad illustration of the vast periods — periods which the boldest imagination can hardly grasp — which countless geological phenomena teach us must have elapsed to work the changes that have taken place in the crust of our globe.

After passing this spot (which bears the same name as a place near Chamouni, having some little resemblance to it, Les Tines), the road descends rapidly till it regains the level of the stream. Here a scene of fresh interest is disclosed. The river that pours through the narrow gorge of Les Tines carries the united waters of two streams, the Upper and the Lower Giffre, which have their confluence a short distance above Les Tines, and enclose between their channels the rich alluvial plain above mentioned — a sort of inverted delta, the base of which is formed by the lowest part of the mountain group dividing the two arms of the river. The little village of Sixt is situated on the left-hand confluent — the Bas Giffre; but though at the distance of only a short quarter of an hour's drive, it is effectually concealed by a turn in the road, which, keeping close to the river, takes a sudden bend round the end of the mountain chain on the left, and pursues a direction nearly at right angles to its former course. In this direction, therefore, the prospect is limited, but on the right is presented a magnificent view of the gorge of the Upper Giffre. This torrent descends from the very heart of the Buet, and sweeping round the western base of the mountain group in front of the spectator, passes at the foot of some of the noblest precipices in the Alps. One glorious peak, which forms the great feature of this view, as of almost every other in the neighbourhood, now comes in sight for the first time; and the most experienced Alpine traveller might rack his memory in vain to call to mind a grander form. It is the Pointe de Salles, the eastern extremity of a mountain range extending to the Aiguille de Varens, just above St. Martin, round whose base winds the high road to Chamouni. In outline it reminds one somewhat of the huge crested crags, like petrified waves of rock, that form the great feature of the view from Leukerbad towards the Ghemmi Pass, but it is beyond all comparison grander and more solemn in form, as well as richer in colouring. The upper part of the mountain is a bare and precipitous structure of naked rock, built tier above tier, rising first gently and then sharply from west to east, and ending in an abrupt precipice of some 1500 or 2000 feet. Nothing can exceed the grandeur of this line of crags, and few that I have seen are equally rich in colour. The rock is a light-brown weather-stained limestone, and seems to have a peculiar aptitude for lighting up with the varying hues appropriate to different times of the day and different states of the atmosphere. In the early dawn I have seen it looking as stern and lifeless, and almost as cold and grey, as the icy brow of Mont Blanc himself; then, as the kindling rays caught its surface and rapidly descended its shaggy sides, violet, then pink, then brilliant, like new gold; beneath the mid-day sun I have seen it looking rich and brown, but most glorious in the glow of declining day, bathed in floods of warmer radiance—now yellow, now all on fire with rosy light, now of a soft sepia tint, and then at length settling once more into the iron hues of dusk. Beneath the serrated ridge is a narrow "swarded shelf," which looks from below so steep that one almost wonders how soil, and herbage, and stunted trees can find a resting-place on such an incline. It projects beyond the eastern base of the precipice, and is itself raised to a height of some thousands of feet above the gorge of the Giffre by a bare perpendicular wall of crag, far more massive than the peak above, and only less imposing because it does not start, like the Pointe de Salles itself, from the level of the clouds. Few persons, however accustomed to the wonders of Alpine passes, could repress a feeling of astonishment on learning that along this wild ledge, beneath the foot and round the nearest extremity of the range of limestone precipices, raised at such a dizzy height, is carried the romantic passage of the Col d'Anterne from Sixt to Servoz. The earlier part of the pass by which the ledge is reached lies in a deep hollow between the base of the Pointe de Salles and a nearer and lower peak of a curious conical form, dotted with firs right up to the summit, and masking the upper part of the valley.

Beside the rugged grandeur of the Pointe de Salles, a fine craggy mass in front of the traveller, occupying, in fact, the larger part of the landscape, has little chance of being duly appreciated. Anywhere else " La Grande Joux " would pass for a noble object. It is a spur of the Buet, its south-western precipices forming one flank of the valley of the Haut Giffre, near the origin of one branch of which it merges in the snow-clad mass of the Buet itself. Its loftier portions are bare and precipitous enough, but lower down it presents a broad expanse of wooded heights; lower still, rich pastures, mingled with patches of arable land, and dotted with straggling orchards, slope down to the alluvial and carefully cultivated plain watered by the streams of the Giffre.

A short descent, and a few minutes' drive by the side of the Giffre — now diminished to a brawling mountain water-course, some twenty yards in width and fordable anywhere — bring the traveller to a long, straggling line of cottages, ending in a little square, graced, like that of Samoëns, by a noble linden tree. At the further end of the square is an oblong enclosure, within which are situated the curé's house, the church, and a long and lofty building parallel to it, and connected with it by a vaulted passage, formerly the Convent of Sixt, (which is still, like Chamouni, called in patois "la Priora,") now the hospitable hostelry of the "Fer à Cheval." A new hall and entrance, or rather restorations of these portions of the old premises, were in contemplation when I was last there (Oct. 1858), and they would be approached through the great gate of the old conventual enclosure, the way to the church also. Up to the time of my last visit, however, you continued for a few yards by the river side, and beneath the convent wall; and just catching one beautiful view of the yet unseen valley of the Bas Giffre, closed in by the glaciers of Mont Rouan and the sharp Pic de Tinneverges, turn in by a little gateway on the left, and, in somewhat primitive fashion, entered the inn through the kitchen.

The "Hotel du Fer à Cheval" has great capabilities. The building is of the most substantial kind, the old staircases, now disused, wide and handsome, the corridors lofty and airy, and the bedrooms excellent. Up to 1858, however, it was not properly organised. Till two or three years ago, the proprietor, Moccand, had only a small portion of the

al has great
of the most sub
now disused, wide
and airy, and
however,
r three year
a small porti

old convent. The kitchen, offices, stabling, and outhouses, with a sort of tap-room, the old refectory, on the ground floor, a rather shabby *salle à manger*, and one good and two indifferent bed-rooms, all opening out of one another, on the first floor, and about the same amount of accommodation on the second, constituted the whole of the premises. In the autumn of 1857, however, he succeeded in buying the whole of the building, which, in 1858, was being gradually brought into habitable condition. A great vaulted corridor, not less than thirty or forty yards in length, runs along the whole length of the building on each floor, out of which open a number of rooms on either hand. On my last visit those on the first floor, on the side of the river, were all habitable. Those on the opposite side of the corridor, against the church, were still filled with lumber, dust, and rubbish, and many were without doors and windows. Vigorous preparations were making, however, for carrying on the work of restoration, and probably by this time a large portion of the building is ready for the reception of visitors. One room which my wife and I occupied for many days in August and September, 1858, I especially commend to the traveller. It is at the end of the house, towards the village, and commands a glorious prospect towards the valley leading up to the Col d'Anterne. I shall not readily forget the sunrises and the moonlight views we have watched from those windows.

The landlord, Moccand, was unfortunately given to sotting, and it was truly deplorable to witness the struggles of his wife—a smart, active, clever Frenchwoman of some fifty years of age — to maintain a little order and regularity in the household. Their only child, a lad of sixteen or seventeen, did not give her much assistance, and the whole service of the house appeared to devolve on Madame Moccand, who presided in the kitchen, and a wonderful maid named "Marie," the gentlest creature that ever was tossed by fortune into such a place, who seemed able to dispense with sleep and food to a greater extent than any other human being I ever met with. Was supper wanted by a belated traveller at ten o'clock at night, Madame Moccand was bustling about as actively as if it were mid-day, frying her excellent trout — the best perhaps in the world — or whipping up a frothing bowl of "œufs à la neigê," while Marie was spreading a clean cloth on the table of the "salle à manger:" was linen to be washed before the morning, Marie was ready to receive it without a murmur, and by the hour named it was sure to be ready: was breakfast needed by some midnight wanderer, like myself, at one or two in the morning, at half-past twelve or half-past one Madame Moccand, as brisk as if she had had a week's repose, was stirring the wood-fire to make the coffee and boil the eggs; and Marie—having passed an hour or two on the bare benches of the tap-room, for fear of oversleeping herself if she gave way to the allurements of bed—pale and worn, and miserably fagged, but with a pleasant smile upon her face, was making all necessary preparations upstairs. With so incomplete a staff, and with a drunken landlord, it was not to be expected that the service of the house should be good. Punctuality is a virtue but ill appreciated at Sixt; but it would be most ungrateful not to say that everything that the united efforts of these two excellent women could accomplish for the comfort and welfare of the guests was most scrupulously performed. The kind folk at the Hotel de Helvétie at Frutigen, are the only people I have met with in my travels who have rivalled Madame Moccand and Marie in thoughtfulness and attention. If Madame had been properly seconded by her husband and her son, they might have had one of the best plain country inns among the Alps. As it was, the poor woman had hard work to keep things straight, and if she had become incapacitated, the place would have gone to rack and ruin at once. I strongly urged upon them the absolute necessity of having a larger staff of servants for the next season, when much more of the house would be thrown open, and I believe they intended to do so. In the winter of 1858, however, Moccand paid the debt of nature, the consequence, if I remember right, of some unusual imprudence. I have not heard how the establishment has fared since, but I have no doubt things have gone on far better since Madame has been free to make her own arrangements, and exercise her own authority. I know that Marie was still there last year.

The " Cuisine Moccand " was not *recherchée*, certainly. It was an odd mixture. Every now and then, as in the œufs à la neige, the chocolate cream, and some other little dishes, it presented glimpses of better things; but uncertainty as to result seemed to be its prominent characteristics. The soup was sometimes excellent, sometimes little better than dishwater; so with the chops, the fried potatoes, the chickens, and most of the other eatables. Still, on the whole, the fare, though plain, was good and wholesome, and such as only fastidious travellers would complain of. Sound and drinkable red wine may be had at a reasonable price, as well as some very fair " Ay Mousseux," and so-called Möet, for those who prefer some form of sparkling wine. The bills I have uniformly found very moderate, and any mistakes that have occurred have invariably been in my favour; and when we have stayed any length of time in the house we have enjoyed a most liberal *pension* for five francs a-day a-piece.

CHAP. II.

> "Majestic circuit, beautiful abyss,
> By nature destined from the birth of things
> For quietness profound."—WORDSWORTH.

> "He held himself for an exempted
> And privileged being, and as if he were
> Incapable of dizziness or fall;
> But now   *   *   *   *   *
> He plunges in unfathomable ruin."
> COLERIDGE.—*The Death of Wallenstein.*

THE FER À CHEVAL, THE FOND DE LA COMBE, AND THE FATE OF JACQUES BALMAT.

THE PIC DE TINNEVERGES.—THE FER À CHEVAL.—THE FOND DE LA COMBE.—A TRAGICAL INCIDENT.—DISAPPEARANCE OF JACQUES BALMAT.—A REVELATION.—THE HUNTER TAKEN OFF HIS GUARD.—MOTIVES OF THE SYNDIC.—THE CHALETS OF BORET.—CATERPILLARS' PARADISE.—LANDSLIPS OF THE TÊTE NOIRE.—THE VAUDRU.

THE village of Sixt, as mentioned in the last chapter, is situated near the extremity of the valley of the Bas Giffre, a few minutes' walk from its junction with the Haut Giffre, which forms with it an obtuse angle; behind this angle lies the massive system of the Buet. The waters of the Bas Giffre are supplied partly, of course, by springs, but mainly by the drainage of the glaciers of the Mont Rouan and others which lie at the back of a remarkable peak or aiguille, called the Pic de Tinneverges, rising abruptly to a height of upwards of 10,000 feet, at a distance of about an hour's walk north-east from Sixt. As you look up the valley this peak forms the most remarkable object in the view. The upper part is a massive pyramid, of broken outline, towering high above the glaciers at its base, very steep and craggy, but dashed here and there with patches of unmelted snow. The lower part belongs to a system of shaggy precipices which guard the southern side of the valley of the Bas Giffre — the right-hand side as you look up the valley — extending in one long line, surmounted at intervals by other and smaller summits, from the Pic de Tinneverges to the block of the Buet itself. Precipices, of less elevation but of equally rugged character, guard the valley on the north side also, so that the Lower Giffre runs in a deep channel or furrow between perpendicular banks of irregular height. The width of the valley from wall to wall may be — I speak at a guess and from memory — from half a mile to a mile and a half. The lower part, however, is filled up with the banks of débris from the heights above, resting at their natural angle of repose, and descending frequently to the river's banks. They are for the most part clothed with woods and thickets — still favourite haunts of the chamois — in which the universal fir is largely mingled with deciduous trees. The lower part of the valley, like the rest of the neighbourhood, is characterised by much natural fertility of soil and luxuriance of vegetation.

Three or four miles above Sixt you come to one of the most curious and interesting scenes of the district. The great wall of precipice forming the southern barrier of the valley suddenly recedes from the course of the river, and curving round in a semicircle, becomes the boundary of an enormous amphitheatre of unparalleled wildness and sublimity. Successive landslips on a colossal scale have half filled up the area beneath with a confused assemblage of low irregular hills, now thickly clad with wood, or brought into more profitable cultivation by the hand of man. Along the whole length of the arc towers an unbroken line of nearly perpendicular precipice, never less than a thousand feet in height, and sometimes considerably higher. This imposing barrier is itself surmounted by a grand chain of still loftier crags, rising terrace upon terrace, till they attain their greatest elevation in the magnificent peak of the Tinneverges — the north-eastern point of the

THE NEW YORK
PUBLIC LIBRARY

ASTOR, LENOX
TILDEN FOUNDATIONS

horse-shoe — and the scarcely less imposing summit of the Tête Noire, about half way between the two extremities of the semicircle; while, further still to the west, the glaciers of the Buet peep over the buttresses of rock, and call to mind the wonders of the upper world of ice and snow. I know few scenes in which the mountains rise so perpendicularly to so great a height. The peak of Tinneverges from this spot presents a remarkably broken and rugged outline; one great block near the top of the mountain detaches itself from the general mass and shoots up in the form of a solitary tower several hundred feet high; and though masses of débris reposing at the foot of each successive terrace of rock inform the mind that the summit is far enough away, the impression produced upon the eye is that of a pinnacle almost above the spectator's head. It is curious to observe how materially the aspect of the mountain is changed by climbing a short distance up the rising ground on the other side of the valley. The eye then takes in the true character of the mountain as a stately edifice solidly built up in accordance with the truest principles of permanence; each story, so to speak, being supported at its base by the most substantial buttresses of earthwork. A sketch taken by my wife, from such a point of view, which lies before me as I write, conveys entirely this impression; yet I well remember how vertical the structure looked from below, as I tried in vain so to plant my camera as to get a satisfactory picture from the truth-telling pencil of the sun.

It is in the spring, however, and in the early summer, that the magnificent amphitheatre of the Fer à Cheval, as it is appropriately named, is seen to its full advantage; for then every notch along the serrated line of crag becomes the birthplace of a waterfall, from the tiny thread of spray which quivers in every breeze, and dances irresolutely down the sombre crag, half dissipated before it lights upon the ground below, to the furious torrent plunging in one bold leap from top to bottom of the deepest precipice, and announcing its presence with a voice that emulates the thunders of the sky. There is no season and no weather in which a number of white streaks may not be seen striping the dark surface of the rock; but it is said that when the winter's snows are thawing rapidly beneath the suns of May and June, their number and volume are extraordinary. Fine waterfalls are characteristic of the neighbourhood of Sixt; so much so, that a notion has long been current, singularly erroneous as it is, that they form the chief attraction of the scenery; and certainly this valley of the Bas Giffre has its full share of them. Several, and among them one of remarkable grace and beauty,— that of La Gouille,— are passed on the way from Sixt to the Fer à Cheval; and the higher part of the valley, above the Fer à Cheval, is graced by several more, though not of so important a character as those which have been already passed.

A tolerable char-road and a gentle ascent make the entrance to the Fer à Cheval easily accessible to even the most delicate of the gentler sex. At this point the road enters a scattered fir wood, which extends across a great part of the valley, and entirely masks its upper end. Here the char-track partially ceases, and there is a short ascent of a steeper character and over rougher ground. The streams from the Fer à Cheval have united in a single channel, and cross the road in an impetuous torrent, which leaves extensive traces of its vigorous action in spring and early summer. Charming little stereoscopic " bits " abound amongst the moss-grown boulders bordering the stream on either hand. Rough as the road is, and swampy though it be occasionally, the char can go half a mile or a mile further, and land its passengers fairly within the Fond de la

Combe, as the wild and secluded recess forming the head of the valley is called. It is a barren plain, two or three miles long, and narrowed to less than half the width of the lower part of the valley, supporting a scanty and reluctant growth of herbage. It is shut in at its upper extremity by a massive barrier of rock, crowned by the glaciers of Mont Rouan, with the sharp Aiguille de Mont Rouan jutting up from amidst them, and jealously guarded on either hand by lofty and converging walls of precipice or of broken crag, interspersed by nearly inaccessible ledges of vegetation. The precipices on the south or right-hand side are particularly steep, and at the same time dotted with innumerable patches of bright green grass, protected from the scorching effect of the mid-day heat upon the produce of such stony ground, by the line of tall cliffs which rise boldly above them, and supply them with a grateful shade. It is astonishing to what difficult heights the industry of the Savoyard peasantry will tempt them in pursuit of grass; and we were told that there is scarcely a spot of verdure along the whole line of crag that is not visited annually for the sake of the scanty hay-crop, which is made up and bound together in bundles, and then rolled down the face of the precipice. Many such places can only be reached by taking the shoes off the feet; one was pointed out to us as the scene of a tragical incident which had happened a year or two previously. A youth, who was helping his father to start a bundle of hay, suddenly lost his footing, and, slipping over the edge of the rock, was dashed to pieces in an instant. He was the second or third of the same family who had met with this fate, yet they still persevered in their dangerous cropping. The wonder is that such accidents do not frequently happen, for most of the tiny hay-fields themselves are on very steep banks, and there is perhaps scarcely any one danger of Alpine travelling so great as that of traversing or descending steep slopes of dry and close-cropped herbage with an unfenced precipice beneath.

The glaciers of the Mont Rouan are interesting to those who care about the great names in Alpine story, as the scene of the tragedy which closed the career of the adventurous Jacques Balmat, the hero of Mont Blanc, perhaps the hardiest and most indomitable mountaineer that ever drew breath, even beneath the shadow of the Alps. He had, unfortunately for himself, contracted a habit of gold-seeking, which kept him poor all his life; and he had long had an idea that in some veins, apparently of carboniferous earth, which streak the calcareous precipices near the glaciers of Mont Rouan, gold-ore might be found. In the month of September, 1834, being then no less than seventy-two years of age, he started, accompanied by a single chasseur of Val Orsine,— one *Pache* by name,— on his perilous tour of discovery. He was seen the following day, in company with the huntsman, making his way towards the head of the Fond de la Combe. Late in the afternoon they reached a solitary hut, called La Cabane des Bergers de Moutons, perched on one of the largest of the patches of grass already mentioned, and here they passed the night. The next day the hunter returned alone, and Jacques Balmat was never seen again. His companion betrayed great reluctance to answer any questions concerning him; and, when pressed, always asserted that they had separated in the morning, Jacques Balmat making his way towards the glaciers, he returning in the other direction, as the old man insisted upon going into places of such danger that he dared not follow him. Of what befel Balmat after they parted, he declared he knew nothing.

The Val Orsine man stuck to his story whenever interrogated, and unsatisfactory as his manner was always felt to be, nothing could be discovered to contradict his account; and there the matter rested till fresh light was thrown upon it by an incident which illustrates curiously the state of society at Sixt, and the nature of the objects of primary importance in the eyes of the village politician. Years after this occurrence, a disclosure was made by a man, who at the time Jacques Balmat disappeared, had been Syndic of the commune, an officer bearing the same title as the chief person of the commune at the present day, but then deriving his authority from the fact of his being the nominee and representative of the central administration, not, as now, from being the free choice of popular election. This person now divulged, for the first time, that the day after Jacques Balmat was last seen, a peasant of his commune had informed him that on the previous day his two children had been playing on the grassy slopes on the northern side of the Fond de la Combe, near the Chalets de Boret, when they beheld a man, who had been apparently creeping along the naked face of the rocks opposite, above a great accumulation of broken blocks of ice which had been pushed over a precipice by the advance of the glacier, suddenly fall and disappear in a chasm between the rock and the ice. Influenced by motives which the reader would scarcely guess, and which it would appear were shared by his informant, the Syndic strictly charged the children never to breathe a syllable of what they had seen, and threatened them with all the undefined terrors of the law if they ever ventured to tell the story to any one else. The children were young, and probably living at a solitary chalet, where they had no one but their parents to talk to, and either forgot or only faintly remembered the incident, or were imbued with a salutary respect for so great a personage as the Syndic, and the secret had been kept to that hour. The ex-Syndic was well aware that the relatives of Balmat had made anxious but fruitless searches for his remains, and that some sort of suspicion of want of candour had fallen upon the Val Orsine hunter, and, whether his conscience at last smote him, that he had suffered him to remain so long under a cloud, or for what other reason does not appear, but he now for the first time told this story to the then Vice-Syndic of Sixt. The Vice-Syndic communicated the intelligence, first to Jean Payot of Chamouni, and afterwards repeated it in the presence of my informant, Auguste Balmat. The children in question were inquired for, but it seemed they had left the neighbourhood. The spot, however, from which the figure had been seen to fall, a little green oasis in the desert of rock, was pointed out; and a fresh expedition was organised, on an extensive scale, from Chamouni. Among the explorers were Auguste Balmat and several other relatives of the deceased, and one Michel Carrier, the artist of the great plan in relief of Mont Blanc known to visitors at Chamouni, and a tolerable draughtsman. With incredible difficulty, and taking the utmost precautions against accident, they succeeded in reaching the green knoll near and at the side of the glacier. Here they found below them a precipice, and at the foot of this the broken masses of ice shot over the edge of the platform on which the glacier rests. Auguste was tied to a rope, but found it impossible to descend the face of the rock, or to get any nearer to the chasm which had received his great uncle. He described it as a black gulf, the bottom of which he could not see, into which a stream issuing from the glacier was thundering, and stones and blocks of ice, broken off as the glacier poured over the ridge, were continually falling. All hope was therefore finally abandoned of the possibility of finding any traces of the great pioneer of Mont Blanc.

Carrier, however, took a sketch of the spot, and the party returned to Chamouni. Some time afterwards he and Auguste Balmat went together to the Val Orsine. When they drew near to the hunter's cottage, Carrier went on alone to the door, and asked Pache if he had seen Balmat, adding, "I expected him somewhere about here; he is gone to seek minerals." The man answered that he had not seen Auguste, but invited Carrier to sit down and wait for him. Half an hour afterwards Balmat came by, as if casually, and asked if Pache had seen Carrier. The hunter insisted on their taking a bottle of wine, to which they assented, on condition that he should come to Val Orsine and dine with them. Accordingly the three adjourned to the inn at Val Orsine, where they sat down to dinner, and Balmat and Carrier took care to ply the old hunter freely with wine. When it had begun to tell upon him a little, and the suspicious reserve he always maintained in the presence of those whom he associated with Jacques Balmat had a little worn away, Carrier, who was sitting beside him, suddenly pulled out the sketch he had taken at the Fond de la Combe, and laid it before him, saying, "Connaissez vous cet image?" The hunter, taken off his guard, started back, exclaiming, "Mon Dieu! voilà où Jacques Balmat est péri!" "What then?" said Carrier; "you know *where* he perished?" The man appeared confused for a moment, and then recovering his habitual caution, said, "No, no, I know nothing about it, but I saw the scene near which I left him, and it struck me as the kind of place he might have fallen down." He then got up, and no entreaties could prevail upon him to stay; and by no artifice could he be induced to approach the subject again.

It is not difficult to understand that an ignorant peasant, fearful of being charged with having had a hand in the death of Jacques Balmat, should have imagined that his safety lay in pretending absolute ignorance of every circumstance connected with his fate; but the conduct of the Syndic, to whom the whole mystery was known, requires to be explained a little more in detail.

It is not easy for a person unfamiliar with the Alps to conceive the importance justly attached by the members of a mountain community to their forests. Not only do they depend upon them, and upon nothing else, for their supplies of fuel and for their building materials, but also for the still more important service of at once breaking up into detached portions the accumulations of the winter snow which falls upon the area they cover, and of forming a protecting barrier against the avalanches hurled from the heights above them. These avalanches bring with them not merely snow, but rocks, stones, and débris, and sweeping over the unprotected mountain sides in prodigious volumes and with incredible velocity, not unfrequently tear off large portions of mould, and kneading it up with their own substance, cover the comparatively level ground, which finally arrests their progress, with a compound of earth and snow. When spring comes round and the snow melts into water, the land is covered with a thick deposit of mud, through which it will perhaps take two or three seasons for the herbage beneath to force its way; so that even if houses, men, and cattle be out of the reach of the avalanche, it may do damage enough to impoverish a whole neighbourhood. Anything, therefore, which tends to the destruction of their forest ramparts, is regarded by the peasantry as a deplorable calamity. Several remarkable instances of the losses inflicted upon the population of a neighbourhood by the destruction of forests to supply fuel for mining purposes, in the southern valleys of the Alps, are recorded in Mr. King's interesting volume, "The Italian Valleys of the Pennine Alps." Jacques Balmat was a noted gold-seeker, and despite his ill-success, enjoyed considerable reputation throughout the communes near to Chamouni as a person of great knowledge and experience on such subjects. The moment the Syndic heard that the children had seen a man fall down the precipice of Mont Rouan, he conjectured that Jacques Balmat, who had been seen in the valley a day or two before, had been searching for gold in that neighbourhood, and that it was he who had met with the terrible fate described by the children. A vague local tradition had long been current, which asserted that gold was to be found in the valley, and that some Swiss adventurers had even made their fortunes by working it; but little heed was paid to the story, and no one had assigned to the popular notion any particular locality. If Jacques Balmat were once known to have selected a definite spot for his researches, his example would be followed; and the discovery which had been frustrated by his tragical death would be accomplished by others. Mines would be opened, vast quantities of wood would be needed to smelt the ore, the interests of the valley would be sacrificed to the influence of persons who could gain the ear of the authorities at Turin, and their forests would be destroyed to feed the cupidity of strange adventurers. Such was the train of thought which passed through the mind of the wary Syndic, and determined him, at all hazards, to suppress every trace of facts which might put future gold-hunters on the right scent. The story seems a strange one, but it is perfectly true, and I shall have occasion to mention before long an incident which occurred to myself, and which strongly illustrates the dread entertained to the present day by the peasantry of Sixt of anything which they fancy may bring about the same catastrophe, and the facility with which they infer that any unwonted project is likely to conduce to it.

It is well worth while to climb from the head of the Fond de la Combe to some of the grassy heights on the left or northern side of the valley. They command magnificent views of the glaciers of Mont Rouan, of the Aiguille de Tinneverges, and of the connected system of the Buet. One at least of these districts of upland pasture supports a considerable group of houses — the Chalets de Boret — the inhabitants of which are occupied almost exclusively in making cheeses. I remember passing through the village in the full heat of a sultry August noon-day, and as usual being unable to procure a draught of milk, though perhaps a hundred cows had been milked there that morning — the whole of their produce being already in process of conversion into cheese. The ascent from the head of the valley to these Chalets of Boret is very beautiful, the path leading for a long distance between thickets of nut-trees, elder bushes, and tangled underwood, and being decorated by a great variety of beautiful wild flowers.

One path by which you may return to the valley is also remarkably wild and picturesque, leading first through such a wilderness of wild raspberries, blackberries, and other mountain fruits, that you must be more or less than man if you can pass quickly through it, and ending in a regular staircase — aptly denominated the Mauvais Pas — cut down the face of the steep buttresses of disintegrated limestone rock, which rise almost perpendicularly from the valley. In some places little waving waterfalls tumble from the heights above, and make the surface slippery beyond description: more than one spot of this kind requires no common precaution in passing it, and before the path is "arranged" (to use the universal phrase of these districts) in spring, the passage must be most dangerous, if not altogether impossible. A track across a similar formation constitutes the main difficulty of the Col de Sagéroux, which leads from the head of this valley to Champéry, at the northern base of the Dent de Midi, and was once so formidable that Balmat told me he had scarcely ever been in such imminent danger as in passing that Col after a shower of rain succeeded by a slight frost. It is now, however, "arranged" so well, as I am told, that an experienced pedestrian may safely undertake it in fine weather with or without a guide.

The whole excursion from Sixt to the Fond de la Combe and back will occupy five or six hours of actual walking; somewhat less if a char be used where practicable: but it is a pity to hurry through such scenery, and any length of time may be profitably employed in this interesting valley. I am told that the glaciers of Mont Rouan are very beautiful and interesting, and well repay the trouble of a visit. They are accessible from the Fond de la Combe, not by climbing up at the end of the valley, but by ascending to the Chalets of Boret, and passing the higher Chalets of Vogalli; you must then quit the track of the Sagéroux, and turning to the right, get behind the Aiguille de Mont Rouan. If the traveller be interested in any branch of natural history, he will find ample material for observation in the rocks, the glaciers, the fossils, the vegetation, and the various forms of insect life. The valley abounds in butterflies: I know nothing of entomology, and can, therefore, speak only as an ignorant observer; but I have seen few valleys north of the great chain which appeared to me so rich in insects, and especially in butterflies, as this arm of the valley of Sixt. When I first visited it in August 1857, there was a portion of the plain of the Fond de la Combe, about a couple of hundred yards long, so covered with the magnificent caterpillars of the sphinx moth, that it was almost impossible to walk across it without crushing scores of them; and, though not in such multitudes, we frequently met with them for a considerable distance above and below this spot. I was unable, where they lay so thick on the ground, to find a single perfect blade of herbage. The euphorbiaceous plants were the objects of their especial affection. It was only after a search of many minutes that I was able to find an unbitten stalk of euphorbia; though the plant was so abundant, that, observing the fondness of the caterpillar for it, we named the place "Caterpillars' Paradise."

I must not forget to mention the magnificent echoes of the Fond de la Combe, which are heard to advantage near a rude bridge over the Giffre, a short distance from the entrance to this portion of the valley. In 1858 we took a small cannon up from Sixt with a couple of charges of powder, and were glad we had done so.

Those who can spare the time would do well, instead of contenting themselves, as people generally do, with looking at the Fer à Cheval from the road up to the Fond de la Combe, to penetrate into its recesses, and examine for themselves the remarkable formation, or series of formations, it presents. The last great land-slip occurred in 1602, when a huge mass detached itself from the Tête Noire; and on so prodigious a scale was the catastrophe, that a village called Entre-deux-Nants*, which is said to have stood close to the Giffre, at a distance of two miles from the mountain (and tradition is generally accurate in such matters), was partially destroyed, and many of the inhabitants killed. Certain it is, from what may be seen at this day, that the débris reached even further than the spot assigned to the village, and now indicated by a cross, the "Croix de Pelly," standing at a point which commands one of the best general views of the Fer à Cheval, and to which an annual pilgrimage is made to offer up the prayers of the neighbourhood against the repetition of such a calamity.

The Pic de Tinneverges would be a worthy object of enterprise to even a practised mountaineer. I have little doubt that the summit may be reached from the back of the mountain as seen from Sixt, though it can hardly be easy of access. One man,

* "Nant" means torrent in the patois of this district.

it is true, offered to conduct me to the top, but I doubted very much, from his manner, whether he had ever been there; and Balmat, who knows the glaciers of Mont Rouan well, told me it was far more difficult than my would-be guide represented it to me. A much easier expedition, quite practicable indeed for a lady, is to the summit of the Vaudru, a mountain of some 8000 or 9000 English feet in height, rising nearly opposite to the Pic de Tinneverges, on the north side of the valley of the Giffre, behind the lofty wall of crags, so that from most parts of the valley of the Lower Giffre it is invisible. I have not ascended it myself, but all accounts concur in representing the excursion as a most interesting one, and the point of view as second only to the Buet.

CHAP. III.

> "We started, and he led me towards the hills,
> Up through an ample vale, with higher hills
> Before us, mountains stern and desolate,
> But in the majesty of distance now
> Set off, and to our ken appearing fair."—WORDSWORTH.

THE LAC DE GERS.

SITUATION OF THE LAKE.—BEAUTIFUL ASCENT.—MOCCAND KEPT IN ORDER.—EXQUISITE WOOD WALK.—VIEW FROM THE GIÉTÀ.—NEGLECT OF WILD FRUITS AMONG THE ALPS.—A DREARY SCENE.—THE LAKE.—THE MONTAGNE DE GERS.—A PICTURE FOR THE STEREOSCOPE.—THE DESCENT.—REMARKS.

I HAVE endeavoured, in the last chapter but one, to give some idea of the scenery lying to the west of Sixt, as it is approached by the high road from Bonneville, and, in the last, of the valley of the Bas Giffre, which rises nearly east of the village, beneath the glaciers of Mont Rouan. I will now ask the reader to explore the district lying to the south-west and south. I do not for a moment pretend to be thoroughly familiar with the mountain groups in either direction. The range on the south, in particular, owing to its broken and indented character, to the quantity and stately growth of its woods, and to the number of streams and waterfalls to which it gives birth, appears to me to offer a better prospect of numerous and varied excursions than almost any mountain chain that I know; but the matchless beauty of the valley of the Haut Giffre, together with circumstances which gave it a special interest in my eyes, exerted such a fascination over me, that I found myself, whether I would or no, constantly wandering towards Les Fonds instead of exploring the recesses of the mountains to the south. Perhaps the most beautiful parts of this southern region are those grouped about the base of the upper tier, so to speak, of the Pointe de Salles. The excursion commonly recommended at Sixt as one of the most interesting, —though I should be far from placing it at the head of the list,—is the ascent to the Lac de Gers, a considerable sheet of water lying in a deep hollow among the mountains, at a height of several thousand feet above the level of Sixt. Passing down the village for a distance of about a hundred yards from the inn, you cross the plank bridge over the Bas Giffre, and strike instantly to the right by a path through the meadows enclosed between the two arms of the Giffre. The object of your expedition now lies straight before you, in a gap between two mountains beyond the Haut Giffre. That to the right is a rounded summit called the Giétà, which rises steeply from the valley by a succession of broken limestone cliffs, masked by innumerable fir trees springing from every ledge, and half hiding the faces of bare crag. That on the left is a singular double-toothed summit, which forms a prominent object in most of the views in this direction from Sixt and from the valley of the Haut Giffre, called the Pointe des Marmottets, or Marmozets. The Lac de Gers lies about midway between these two mountains, but much further back than either. There is nothing from below to excite a suspicion of its existence, or to indicate that the gap between the two mountain groups ends in the secluded recess in which the lake is situated. The path across the meadows leads, in about twenty minutes, to a little bridge over the Haut Giffre, its junction with the Bas Giffre being about half a mile lower down the river. It is a much more considerable stream than the Bas Giffre, and owes a large portion of its volume to the melting of ice and snow, as is evinced by its muddier aspect. The approach to this bridge

opens some fine views of the
Giltra, and shows to … …
and majestic proportions of … … …
Crossing the bridge you … … … …
a spur of the Giétroz … … …
towards a stream which dr… … … …
forms in its rapid descent a … … …
…lis. After a very few minutes … …
little cluster of chalets, sur… … …
growth of wood, comprising fir … …
a… nu… as well as beech… …
ciduous forest trees. From … …
bridge by which the stream … …
is crossed—a short half hour's wa… …
…ally exquisite. The track n… … …
…times by actual steps cut in … …
…backwards and forwards —now …
…us plantation of beeches, now … … …
…derwood, now trembling on the b… of … …
d profound precipice, fringed with t… … …
:— one wall of a narrow gorge, down which the
torrent takes one of its grandest leaps. There are
one or two places where, by clambering a few steps
down from the path,—a descent requiring a good deal
…aution,—you may look into a tremendous …
d filled with the tumultuous cataract. The s…

opens some fine views of the valley of the Haut Giffre, and shows to advantage the grand outline and majestic proportions of the Pointe de Salles. Crossing the bridge you begin immediately to ascend a spur of the Giétà, gradually working to the left, towards a stream which drains the Lac de Gers, and forms in its rapid descent a series of beautiful waterfalls. After a very few minutes' climb, you reach a little cluster of chalets, surrounded by a sturdy growth of wood, comprising fruit-trees — as cherries and nuts — as well as beeches, elms, and other deciduous forest trees. From this point to a little bridge by which the stream from the Lac de Gers is crossed — a short half hour's walk — the scenery is really exquisite. The track mounts very steeply, sometimes by actual steps cut in the rock, and winds backwards and forwards — now close to a glorious plantation of beeches, now amongst brush and underwood, now trembling on the brink of an abrupt and profound precipice, fringed with twisted pine trees — one wall of a narrow gorge, down which the torrent takes one of its grandest leaps. There are one or two places where, by clambering a few steps down from the path, — a descent requiring a good deal of caution, — you may look into a tremendous chasm, half filled with the tumultuous cataract. The slope of the walls of rock conceals the bottom of the chasm, but the spot on which you stand actually overhangs the fall; and as you cannot tell how much farther the white sheet of foaming spray may reach, the grandeur of the scene is heightened by the sense of mystery. The roar is tremendous, and it requires a steady head to gaze without discomfort into the seething and agitated mass below.

The view from the little bridge itself is extremely picturesque, as you look up the stream and see fall after fall leaping towards you in sheets of white foam, dwindling as the eye travels upwards, to silver threads—a track of glistening light amidst the rich and varied green of forest and pasture. I had with me, when I went to the Lac de Gers, a camera for taking stereoscopic pictures, and I saw few spots on the way so tempting as this; but a lady was of the party, and her horse was carrying my apparatus. We had started from Sixt as late as seven o'clock, and on these steep slopes, with their somewhat eastern exposure, the heat was already very great, so that it was not convenient to stop for photography, and I was obliged to content myself with thinking how beautiful the scene would look in the camera. Having crossed the bridge, and having the stream now on our right, we climbed, by one of the steepest bridle paths I ever saw, along the ridge of a kind of natural embankment — a regular "Alpine buttress"— which fell away on either side of us. For about half an hour our way lay upon the bare shoulder of turf, where there was not one tree to give a momentary shelter from the burning sun; and a more sultry little walk I have seldom taken. We were glad to press on to a chalet at the top of the turf slope, where we saw a sycamore tree, beneath which we could enjoy the blessings of shade, and accordingly we urged Moccand's stout little mare to a pace which did not distress her, but caused her owner, who had been indulging a little too freely in "hairs of the dog that bit him," the greatest annoyance. He was soon distanced, but kept up a brisk cannonade of mingled abuse and remonstrance addressed to us, the intervals being filled up by a running fire of curses muttered to himself. When he came up to us beneath the sycamore, he was inclined to be so rough in his language that I was obliged to hint at the possibility of my having to inform against him at head-quarters. Moccand, when not in his cups, was kept well in hand at home, and the threat of telling Madame of his conduct wrought an instant and most satisfactory change in his demeanour. He began to apologise on the ground that he had been afraid we should go wrong (there being but one path!) and endeavoured to atone for his rudeness by the most obsequious civility.

We had now reached a height of a thousand or fifteen hundred feet above Sixt, and were upon the ridge bounding the little valley, at the bottom of which lay the stream we were to follow to its source. Quitting our sycamore shade we changed it for that of a beautiful wood, through which we wound, on nearly the same level, for about a quarter of an hour. For this short distance the path is one of the most exquisite I remember among the Alps. Scattered thickets of stunted trees and underwood deepened, as we advanced, into a thick mass of forest trees of variegated foliage, through which the burning rays of the sun could barely struggle, except where some opening in the wood gave us a glance into the world without; each new view presenting a fresh picture, set in a graceful frame of nature's own beautiful workmanship. As we advanced, the wood became ever denser, and moss-grown boulders lay thick on either side of our path, while a plentiful undergrowth of bilberries and wild raspberries and strawberries certainly did not detract from the charms of the scene. The increasing roar of water soon told us that we were not far from the stream, and presently we emerged from the wood and found ourselves by the side of a picturesque saw-mill, close to the head of this section of the valley. Just above the saw-mill was a steep wall of crags, the parent of another grand cascade, whence the water fell quickly down a rough and broken bed choked with rocks, and abounding in exquisite little pools and rapids. Again did I long for the camera, and again did the thought of the increasing heat urge us forward. At this spot you recross the stream, and have then the choice of two paths to the Lac de Gers. It is much the shortest route to climb by a very steep and rugged track — it can hardly be called a path — amongst the fir woods lying to the right of the waterfall; and this ascent again is of rare beauty — but it is impracticable for horses, and the other way, though involving a long round, leads to a very fine point of view well worth the extra trouble. We took the longer way, as we had the horse with us, and working back along the opposite side of the valley to that by which we had latterly been ascending, made straight for a little depression between the Giétà and the rest of the range on our left. The steep slopes both above and below the path were in many places tilled for corn; the parched soil was covered with a short dry stubble and burned our feet as we walked over it: the aspect is southern, not a tree cast its shade across our path, and there was not a breath of air. Had this part of the ascent been long we should have had quite enough of it; the whole excursion, however, is not on a great scale, and in about half an hour from the saw-mill we reached the neck of the range, where a continuation of our path, leading down the other side of the Giétà, would have conducted us by an easy descent to Samoëns. The top of the Giétà rose still above us in gentle undulating slopes of rich pasture ground; and leaving Moccand and his horse under the shade of one of a little cluster of chalets close to the path, we wandered onwards to the summit. It was much further than it looked, but that we did not regret, as every step we took projected us further into the valley and increased the excellence of our point of view. On a small scale it reminded me in some respects of the Gumihorn near Interlaken. Like that remarkable mountain, it towers above the point of confluence of several valleys, and has a raking view of each. The valleys of the Haut and Bas Giffre are both more or less commanded by the Giétà, while the straighter valley by which their united waters flow down to join the Arve, lies open throughout nearly the whole of its length. The Vaudru, the Pic de Tinneverges, the Pointe de Salles, and the Buet are conspicuous objects in the view, and further to the right the great glaciers clustered about the Aiguilles du Tour and d'Argentieres call to mind agreeably all the countless delightful associations connected with the names of Mont Blanc and Chamouni. Mont Blanc himself was hidden by the lofty form of the Pointe de Salles. The part of the scene which old Moccand had been especially anxious we should notice was the bird's-eye view of Sixt, and he begged us particularly to observe how large the old convent looked, as compared with the other buildings in the place. He was evidently gloating over the thought that it was all his own.

We soon descended again to the place where we had quitted the path, and now turned our backs upon the Giétà, and took to a broad and well-beaten track, quite practicable for the rough chars of the country, which the very considerable produce of the Montagne de Gers renders it almost necessary to bring up from Samoëns for the purposes of transport. The Giétà is nearly as high as the Lac de Gers, so that we had not much more climbing to do. For about half an hour our route lay through a beautiful forest of straight and shapely firs, affording a most welcome protection from the hot sun; they were succeeded by a knoll of rising ground which we felt no doubt was the barrier of the lake, as we saw no higher ground beyond it. It was a strange, wild, desolate spot, dotted with withered firs and grey mouldering stumps, a kind of "blasted heath," except that it was covered with a marvellous profusion of bilberry bushes of the most excellent quality and in full bearing. Of course no use is made of them, though there is fruit enough to be had for the gathering, not only to supply a welcome addition to the meagre dessert of the hotel dinners, but to make an unlimited quantity of excellent tarts, jams, and preserves. A bushel might be plucked and brought down from the mountains for a franc, or even much less, if children were employed to pick them; but the bilberry is utterly neglected among the Alps, although at such places as Chamouni and Zermatt, where the supply of wild strawberries and raspberries is totally inadequate to the demand, it would afford a most grateful substitute to many a tired and thirsty pedestrian, to whom fresh fruit would be the most delicious and wholesome refreshment that could be offered. Chamouni, however, is a marvel of incongruities. It boasts the best guides among the Alps, while, by its abominable regulations, it nearly drove those who would employ them to other scenes of adventure; it elects the "oldest and most desartless men" to manage the affairs of the corporation of guides; and though it is close to inexhaustible supplies of the best ice in the world, and full of excellent cooks, the cheap and wholesome luxury of an ice, which might be flavoured either with syrups or with fresh bilberries, cannot be had for love or money. As we had a juster appreciation of the bilberry than the natives, we called a halt, and flinging ourselves on the ground made the best use we could of an opportunity made doubly agreeable by the heat of the day.

Having thus availed ourselves of "the good the gods provide," we continued on our way, and arrived in a few moments at the top of the knoll. What was our surprise to find no lake behind! but a great basin a couple of miles across, apparently once the bed of a lake, but now a bare expanse of pasture land, dotted with abundance of boulders, large and small, from the mountains on either hand, traversed by the sinuous bed of the stream we had not yet hunted to its origin, and blocked at the upper end by a long low bank almost like an artificial mound. A few black, comfortless-looking chalets, built of untrimmed stones and surrounded with the usual sea of filth, were scattered about the course of the stream; a few dun-coloured cattle were listlessly chewing the cud in various parts of the pastures; on either side of the stream was such an accumulation of stones and débris as almost to conceal its waters: the grass had been eaten down as close as it could be, and the stunted herbage left by the cattle was parched and withered by the sun. In fact, a more cheerless, arid, and inhospitable prospect it is not easy to imagine. We crossed the dreary waste as quickly as we could, and climbing the bank at the upper end, came upon another and larger village of black and gloomy chalets, with their usual muddy accompaniments, and after a short descent found ourselves on the banks of the Lac de Gers.

It is curious enough to find a large body of water at so great a height and so far back in the heart of the mountains; otherwise there is nothing particularly interesting in the ending of the excursion. The lake is about a quarter of a mile in its extreme length, and from two to three hundred yards in width. On the north-western or right-hand side, as you come from Sixt, the deepness of its colour, and the steepness of the mountain slopes above it, would lead to the conclusion that it was of considerable depth; the opposite slope is more gentle, and the bed of the lake shelves very gradually down, for a considerable distance. At its upper end is a great patch of sand, a sort of delta formed by the mountain torrent which feeds it, and no doubt covered with water when the lake is unusually high. Here the inclination of the bed is very gentle indeed; in bathing, we found bottom thirty feet from the edge of the water, and a queer, shallow, flat-bottomed tub, furnished with two paddles, of very different shapes and sizes — the only craft that navigates the waters of the lake — which we borrowed from the villagers, and which did not draw six inches of water, grounded several yards out. On the side next the village, the lake appears to be much deeper. The bottom is covered with boulders, very painful to the naked feet; but there we were out of our depth almost immediately. The waters of this lake, like that of the Lac d'Anterne, are of a very peculiar deep green, such as I have rarely seen elsewhere. The Lac d'Anterne must be of immense depth, and in places — even under a bright sun — is very nearly the colour of the bottles generally used in Sardinia for the common wines, when held up to the light. The Lac de Gers is not of so deep a hue, but it must be far shallower than the Lac d'Anterne. I remember a little tarn, not fifty yards long, but apparently of great depth — by the side of the Glacier d'Orny, within a few paces of the Chapelle d'Orny, which is of the same curious colour, but quite as dark as the Lac d'Anterne. The lakelet of Orny, like the Lac d'Anterne and the Lac de Gers, is fed chiefly by snow-water; for though close to the side of the glacier, it is separated from it by a huge wall of moraine, and just above it lies a great patch of snow, the accumulation of the avalanches of spring, which, when I passed over it in the middle of September, was lying still unmelted. The temperature of the Lac de Gers, however, was much higher than I should have expected; we did not find it at all too cold for comfortable bathing.

The scenery of the Lac de Gers is as monotonous and uninteresting as it is possible to conceive. The left-hand bank is clad with firs — some of them very noble trees — but the right-hand bank is comparatively bare, and beyond the herbless expanse of *débris* at the upper end of the lake is a deep prolongation of the valley, enclosed between two steep slopes of naked mountain-side, unbroken by a tree or even a prominent rock. Across the head of this valley, a pass, which must be beautiful enough on the other side, leads to the village of Maglan on the Chamouni Road, between Cluses and St. Martin. Here, however, no snowy peak rises beyond the head of the valley; neither crag, nor precipice, nor broken outline relieves the dull uniformity of the scene: the only encouraging feature in the prospect is the distant view of the mountains near the Fer à Cheval, seen over the low stony bank that dams up the waters of the lake, and reminding you that you may find your way back to the brighter world you have left. But for all this, the Montagne de Gers is far more precious in the eyes of a native than the grandest scene that rock and glacier could furnish forth; for it is one of the richest and most extensive pastures of the district, a famous nursery for young cattle and horses, and not less renowned for the amount and excellence of the dairy produce.

Dull as the scene was, we stayed near the lake till the heat of the day was past, and then turned homewards. We sent the horse on by the circuitous path by which we had ascended; and, in returning across the dreary basin below the Lac de Gers, kept along the course of the stream, leaving the bilberry knoll on our left. In the hollow between the foot of this knoll and the mountain on our right, we came upon another saw-mill, most beautifully situated by the side of the clear rivulet. A thousand springs of crystal water, welling out of the ground underneath or beside the stream, were pouring forth their contributions, a pine forest lay beyond it, and in the distance, some fifteen miles away, rose the Pic de Tinneverges, with a mass of glaciers and smaller snow-clad peaks grouped about the base of his bold sugar-loaf summit. I had shouldered the camera when we parted with the horse, and felt myself well rewarded for the trouble of bringing it up by meeting at last with an exquisite little picture just suited for the stereoscope. The dashing rivulet, with its broken, stony bed, the rough and dripping troughs along which the water was carried to the mill, the stacks of sawn timber, some arranged in the form of an inverted V, others built up in squares, each presenting those alternating lines of light and shade which always look beautiful in photography, backed by the jagged tops of the pine forests, with the white glaciers and the sharp peak in the distance, made just such a composition as possesses all the elements of an effective stereoscopic picture. It was the last I was destined to take for some time, for I incautiously sat down on my ground-glass focusing screen and smashed it to atoms. Ground glass is not to be got at Sixt or Samoëns, and it took Balmat and Cachat nearly three whole days of wet weather to grind a suitable face to a piece of common window glass. Their manufacture, however, served me for the rest of my journey.

The descent through the pine wood to the lower saw-mill need not occupy many minutes. At first there is a path lying beneath noble trees and skirted by tangled underwood. Presently you reach the skirts of the forest, and make your way by a rough scramble over very steep and broken ground, commanding beautiful views of the rich pastures and fertile valley far beneath, till you come to the foot of the fall by which the stream has made its bolder descent from the top of the crags above. I think I was told that a path of some sort exists, avoiding by a circuit the roughest places, but we did very well without it. The rest of the descent was easily and rapidly accomplished, and without hurrying ourselves we reached Sixt in about two hours and a half from the time we quitted the Lac de Gers.

We loitered so much that I hardly know exactly how long the excursion would occupy if time were not so spent; but it is one advantage of such short expeditions, that there is plenty of time to stop on the way and enjoy to the uttermost every scene and object of interest. It is useful, however, to know the amount of actual walking or riding involved;

and I think that from two hours to two hours and a half would be ample time to reach the Lac de Gers from Sixt, taking the short scramble from the lower saw-mill; the circuit that must be made by a horse or mule will require about three quarters of an hour more. A couple of hours are amply sufficient for the descent. Every one, however, who makes the excursion should climb to the top of the Giétà, and make his way for a short distance down the side towards Sixt, where he will come to the edge of a precipice and look down upon the village. It is a far more complete and interesting view than that from the rounded knoll forming the actual summit. I cannot, however, see that much is gained, unless some special object of scientific research be in view, by extending the trip to the lake itself. The picturesque interest of the excursion is confined entirely to the earlier portions, and ceases at the bilberry knoll—afterwards, there is hardly anything to please the eye. Several parts of the ascent from Sixt have attractions of no common order; but on the whole, I think I prefer any of the other excursions from Sixt described in this volume, to the present one. Above all, start early enough for this ascent. The turf slopes are long and fully exposed to the morning sun, and by eight o'clock on a warm

August morning the heat is almost unbearable. Such at least was our experience, though I ought to say that when I went to the Lac de Gers, it was the first excursion of the season for us, made the day after our arrival from England; so that we were likely to feel it more than we should have done afterwards. I have only to add that no guide is necessary. I do not think any one who bore in mind that the lake lies in the hollow he had before him, when he first left the bridge at Sixt, could lose his way; and though it is most convenient to make use of the path, there would be little difficulty in ascending or descending anywhere.

CHAP. IV.

> "The spot was made by nature for herself,
> The travellers know it not ;   *   *   *
>   *   *   *   But it is beautiful,
> And if a man should plant his cottage near,
> Should sleep beneath the shelter of its trees,
> And blend its waters with his daily meals,
> He would so love it, that in his death-hour
> Its image would survive amongst his thoughts."
> WORDSWORTH.

THE VALLÉE DES FONDS AND THE "EAGLE'S NEST."

COURSE OF THE HAUT GIFFRE.—SALVAGNY.—THE POINTE DE SALLES.—" LE ROUGET" AND "LA PLEUREUSE."—LUXURIANT VEGETATION.—LA CROIX D'ESPÉRIT.—CURIOUS STRATIFICATION.—FALLS OF "LES JOUBAS."—THE PATH OF THE AVALANCHE.—PRECIPICES OF THE BUET.—LES FONDS.—MAGNIFICENT VIEW FROM THE PLATEAU.—LOVE AT FIRST SIGHT.—MANAGEMENT OF COMMUNAL AFFAIRS.—PROPOSAL TO PURCHASE.—OPPOSITION OF THE CURÉ.—POSITION OF THE PRIESTS IN SARDINIA.—DIFFICULTIES STARTED.—THE OPPOSITION PARTY THE STRONGER.—COUNT D'ELIA.—A SECOND DELIBERATION AND A CASTING VOTE.—THE COUNT INSULTED.—MEMORIALS AND COUNTER-MEMORIALS.—THE ROYAL ASSENT OBTAINED.—MONSIEUR DE BERGÖENS.—OUR VISIT IN 1858.—DEPUTATIONS.—A SERENADE.—SALUTES FIRED.—HOSPITALITIES.—GENEROUS BEHAVIOUR OF ALL PARTIES.—THE "EAGLE'S NEST" NAMED.—THE CHALET PLANNED.—OUR NEIGHBOURS AND THEIR CORDIALITY.

THE excursion I shall attempt to describe in the present chapter is a very short one. I have often reached the Chalets des Fonds from Sixt in an hour and a half; but it is at once so grand and so full of softer beauty, it presents so many varied aspects of the finest mountain scenery, that I feel almost disposed to lay down the pen and abandon the effort in despair. I have little fear of exaggerating its attractions, for after having visited it nearly a score of times and spent day after day in passing and repassing the same spots — after having seen it in sunshine and in shade, in fine weather and in wet, by the light of moon and stars, by the first faint rays of the early dawn, in the blaze of noonday, and in the softer radiance of sunset, it seems to me still, as it did the first hour I beheld it, utterly unprepared for its charms, simply the most attractive scene I know — even amongst the wonders of the Alps a very miracle of beauty.

The Haut Giffre, which flows through the Vallée des Fonds, takes its rise in the very heart of the Buet, at a distance of two or three hours' walk from Sixt. From its origin, it sweeps in a westerly direction against the Pointe de Salles — the easternmost extremity of the Chaine des Fys—whence it is turned off and flows nearly north, or a little to the west of north; so that from its source to its junction with the Bas Giffre, close to the village of

Sixt, it forms a kind of irregular elongated semi-ellipse. During the greater part of its course the mountains hem it closely in, so that the path is obliged to follow very nearly the windings of the river. For about half an hour's walk after leaving Sixt, however, the country on the right bank of the stream is of a different character, and the precipitous heights of the upper part of the valley tone down into rolling hills, and finally merge in a little plain enclosed between the two arms of the river. The path from Sixt leads first across the bridge over the Bas Giffre, and past some rough broken-down stone buildings, the memorials of an adventurous speculation in the shape of iron-works, to which a company of sanguine gentlemen once looked with exalted hopes, but which resulted in burying their fortunes deeper than the ore which they were unlucky enough to have found; then, keeping at a distance of more than half a mile from the river, it winds over the gentle acclivities that succeed to the steeper slopes and ruder heights above, till it is compelled by the narrowing of the valley to draw near to the stream. The borders of the flowing drapery with which nature clothes the mountain sides are commonly wrought of her richest materials and dyed in her brightest colours; and the northern base of the system of the Buet forms no exception to the general rule. Close beneath the lowest of the limestone crags nestle dark forests of pine, soon mingled with the variegated foliage of deciduous trees; further down, sloping more gently towards the stream, are pleasant pasture lands, and lower still the rich and carefully cultivated fields which sink finally into the plain — sprinkled with fruit-trees, dotted with substantial chalets, and showing all the signs of a grateful appreciation by man of the bounties of the soil. From this part of the route a series of cascades, fed from the Lac de Gers, and the fine fall of the Grand Nant, nourished in the valleys of the double-toothed Pointe des Marmottets, are important and beautiful features of the scene. The roar of their waters may often be distinctly heard, wafted by the wind across the valley.

Two villages are passed; the first not exceeding the dimensions of a petty hamlet, the second, by name Salvagny, considerably larger than Sixt, and the richest village in the commune, though dirty enough, in all conscience. The chalets, though very plain, are of unusual size; nearly every house is built wholly or in part of stone, and some of the most prejudiced and impracticable men in the world are to be found among its inhabitants. It boasts a church whose glittering spire is a conspicuous object from many an elevated point of view in the neighbourhood. The bold summit of the Pointe de Salles comes into view not long after leaving Sixt, but it is not till Salvagny has been passed that the full grandeur of its majestic proportions can be realised. The screen of houses, trees, and rising ground which has hidden the lower portion of its massive form, is now withdrawn; and, though a pleasing foreground is wanting to complete the picture in an artistic point of view, nothing can be more striking than the aspect of its tremendous precipices, now unmasked from the very base of the mountain to the summit of its loftiest crag.

Within a few feet of the last house in the village you come unexpectedly on the banks of a torrent, reprobated by the universal voice of the neighbourhood as *des plus méchants*. It rises beneath the rocks of the Grande Joux, the last summit in that part of the Buet range which is prolonged towards Sixt, and receives the drainage of a large area. A great portion of the space which feeds it must consist of surfaces of the steepest inclination, for the prodigious volume of water it is sometimes charged with could not be accounted for unless the supplies were collected with extreme rapidity. It must also be fed from a stony district, for the size of its swollen stream is not more remarkable than the quantity of stones it brings down. The bed of the water-course close to Salvagny cannot be less than fifty yards across, at the very lowest estimate. In the summer, during fine weather, this space is dry from side to side, with the exception of two or three insignificant rivulets, which there is not the slightest difficulty in crossing dry-shod; but the wider channel is completely filled with a slate-coloured mass of worn and rounded stones, rarely of any great size, over which the traffic of the summer hardly succeeds in impressing a definite path. Lower down the débris spreads out on each side into a desolate, herbless expanse, of vast extent, and in shape like a fan, from whose barren surface every trace of life and vegetation has long been swept away. As the reader would expect from this lateral expansion of the débris, the torrent has now reached a nearly level spot, where its destructive force is so far expended that a belt of fir wood close to the Giffre is left standing, and screens that river from the sight.

Up to this " mauvais torrent," the path we have been pursuing, not only leads to Les Fonds, but is the commencement of the road to the Col d'Anterne. From this point the two paths diverge:

that to the Col d'Anterne turns to the right and descends, as if making directly for the base of the Pointe de Salles; at the distance of about twenty minutes' walk it comes upon the river, which it crosses by a romantic bridge, and then ascends in the lateral valley running back from the Giffre, and lying between the Pointe de Salles on the left, and the Pointe des Marmottets on the right. Our path to Les Fonds begins at once sharply to ascend the mountain side on the left; and here the characteristic beauties of the excursion commence. The first two or three hundred yards are bare enough, and towards the middle of the day the heat is often very great indeed, but every onward step brings you nearer to the Pointe de Salles, and reveals more fully its vast proportions, and the majesty of its rugged form. The notch at its north-western base, forming the valley by which the steep ascent to the Col d'Anterne begins, is likewise an object of increasing interest, as the increasing height gained by the spectator gives him a more commanding view of the details of its scenery. He cannot fail to observe the great beauty of its lower slopes, partly carpeted with the bright verdure of Alpine pastures, partly clothed with rich woods, composed, like all those along the banks of the Giffre, not only of pine and larch, but also of such forest trees as we are more accustomed to at home, whose presence, with their more varied forms and richer foliage, so greatly enhances the charms of woodland scenery. Nature does wisely to guard her most attractive scenes by lofty barriers of impassable crag, such as shut in, on either side, this well protected valley. Nor must I omit to mention that it is graced by two exquisite waterfalls, totally different in character, but each most beautiful of its kind. The lower, the Rouget, is justly considered the finest cascade in this region of waterfalls; it is not only of great height and volume, but graceful in form, and surrounded by every accessory that can enhance its romantic effect.

The other fall for which this valley is noted is much higher up, and contains a smaller body of water; but it flows in a broad stream down a series of smooth slabs of rock, broken by numberless ledges; the whole system not perpendicular, but inclined at a high angle, so that there is no spout or shoot of water, as in most cases, but a broad network of skeins of silver threads, each gathered up at its origin and shaken out loosely as it makes its voiceless way down the slab of polished rock, till it meets a fresh ledge, and the scattered filaments are brought together again and shed afresh over the next surface of descent. The result is a gentle, uncomplaining, almost noiseless pouring forth of trickling streamlets, to which the peasantry have given the appropriate and poetical title of "La Pleureuse." Even at the distance at which it is seen from the path to Les Fonds, the peculiar character of the cascade is perfectly distinguishable; it is, however, from the ascent to the Col d'Anterne that it is best seen, as the Pleureuse is the culminating point of the path in this direction; just beneath it, the track turns sharply to the left, and winds back along the steep and grassy shelf separating the lower from the upper precipices of the Pointe de Salles.

Our path does not linger long on the bare mountain side. In a very few minutes the skirt of a deep pine forest is gained; and here one begins to appreciate the difference between the vegetation of the valley of Sixt and that of almost every other Alpine valley that I know. Generally speaking, but little verdure is to be seen beneath the thick foliage of a fir wood; the dry twigs, the withered leaves, and the decaying cones, make a soft and yielding bed of half-formed mould, whence one could fancy that a luxuriant vegetation ought to spring: but it is not so; every traveller who has visited the Montanvert or the Flégère, or ascended the Cramont, knows that beneath the fir-woods he generally sees a drab-coloured soil, scarcely more than dotted with an occasional spot of herbage; but here, in this valley of the Giffre, the trunks of the fir-trees pierce through a tapestry of the richest and softest green. Mosses and ferns grow with the utmost vigour and freedom, and cover every inch of ground not actually occupied by the boles of the trees. When the sun is shining brightly, and pierces here and there through the thick foliage of the wood, it is impossible to say how beautiful are the effects of the chequered light and shade, the alternations of the brightest emerald and of the deepest sea-green, as one stands above and gazes down the glades and vistas of the forests, the aisles and colonnades with which Nature herself adorns the wayside temples she rears on every hand to the great Author of this beautiful universe. There is one spot, just after the fir-wood is reached, where the path passes close to a large boulder, so exquisitely covered with a soft thick carpeting of moss, and itself so excellently shaped for purposes of repose, that I was seldom able to pass it without yielding to the temptation of laying myself at full length upon its green surface and enjoying the luxury of a couch that fitted exactly into every part of the frame which seemed to need support.

The mountains now close in on the left, and boulders which have rolled from above begin to be of not unfrequent occurrence; the prospect is narrowed to the vistas formed by successive stretches of the path itself, bounded by the fir-wood on the right, and on the left by broken ground strewn with rocks, dotted with stunted beeches, and surmounted by low walls of limestone crag, but always ending in the towering form of the Pointe de Salles, so lofty as to seem to belong to another world. At length a little cross, called La Croix d'Espérit, is reached, where a pile of two or three logs invites the wayfarer to take a moment's rest. It is only a short hour from Sixt, and is half-way to Les Fonds, but the peasants have a trick of stopping here, and the scene is so very beautiful that we readily fell into the habit. The trees have been cut away, or cease to grow, for a short space below the cross, so that the view of the Pointe de Salles, the Rouget, and the valley whence its waters come, and of the Pointe des Marmottets, is uninterrupted. The Giffre is not visible, being at a great depth below, at the foot of what you would suppose to be a precipice, were it not that the tops of the fir-trees are

visible just beneath your feet. Looking back, there is a pleasing glimpse of the rich country below Salvagny, and of the mountain ranges converging upon Sixt.

A quarter of a mile or so beyond La Croix d'Espérit, the fir-wood comes to an end, and is replaced by beautiful slopes of bright grass-land. It is here that we get, perhaps, the most interesting of all the varied views of the Pointe de Salles; for we are now opposite to it, and can see how very curious as well as how grand a mountain it is. The stratification of the vast and solid wall of dark rock which forms, so to speak, its lowest story, is most remarkable. The materials of which it is built are disposed with wonderful regularity in long strata of parallel curvature, starting from the left, running straight across the face of the precipice in a horizontal direction, bending gently round before they reach the right-hand extremity of the rock, and then folded back upon themselves. They thus form a system of concentric curves, each of which is about two-thirds of a tolerably regular ellipse with its longer axis horizontally placed; it is, in fact, in mathematical language, a family of concentric ellipses, cut off by a vertical line through one of the conjugate foci. The parallel bands look as if they had been forced upwards by a thrust from some wedge-shaped mass, and then gently laid over on their sides, with such care as not to interfere in the least with the regularity of their formation.

The valley of the Giffre now bends to the left, and as our path winds over the shoulder of the mountain, a view of no common magnificence opens upon us. When we look towards the opposite side of the valley, the Pointe de Salles, which has hitherto been the prominent object on our left, now takes its place on the right hand of the picture, while the left is occupied by the extremity of a dark and massive mountain range presented to the spectator "end on," and running backwards in a direction nearly parallel with the Chaine des Fys, of which the Pointe de Salles is the eastern peak. These two points might be likened to the bastions at each extremity of a face of fortification, and the *curtain* connecting them is a lower sweep of mingled precipice and wood, presenting one of the wildest nooks to be found among the Alps. Abrupt walls of dark crag rise one above another to a height not perhaps exceeding two or three thousand feet, but from the proximity of our point of view having all the grandeur of much vaster proportions. Each successive tier of nature's masonry rests on a slope of earthwork, but there is a striking contrast between the two halves of the picture. On the left, the faces of crag are lower, and form a less important feature in the scene; it is not till a considerable height has been attained that they assume any grand proportions: the lower slopes are profusely clad with forest trees of stately growth and variegated foliage, while above, the mountain breaks away into perpendicular faces of sombre crag, marked by strangely-contorted lines of stratification. On the right, the scene preserves the barren and precipitous character which belongs to the Pointe de Salles; and the wooded slopes on the left give way to a series of irregular banks of black shale,— looking like the ruins of a mountain — separated by lofty walls of bare crag. The extremes of desolation and of richness are thus brought together in magnificent contrast; near the banks of the Giffre, even the gloomy masses of black débris cannot refuse to wear the cheerful livery of the forest green. Far above, from the barrenest and most distant point in the amphitheatre, a beautiful mountain torrent — the outpouring of the Lac d'Anterne —shoots over a wall of rock, and finds a momentary hiding-place in the broken débris at its base; an instant afterwards it comes forth again, and plunges with a bolder leap down a loftier precipice; it is lost again, and once more reappears on the brink of a third face of rock. Before it reaches the Giffre, it has disappeared and come to light again no less than five or six times; thus marking its descent by a series of beautiful waterfalls — the Cascades de la Joubas — which not only enliven the scene by their irregular disposition, their sparkling aspect, and their dancing outlines, but by their diminishing perspective give an almost magical air of distance and vastness to the scenery. Often as I have passed along this path, I have seldom been able to refrain from stopping for some minutes to take in the full charms of this scene of wild and varied beauty.

From this point the valley becomes narrower, and the scenery assumes a wilder and more gorge-like character. The slopes along which our path is carried become steeper and steeper; above and below us are charming alternations of beech coppices and strips of grass land, as trim and closely shaven as an English lawn. The wall of limestone precipices crowning the heights on our left, at once increases in height, and draws nearer to our path, with every onward step. Romantic hollows seam the mountainside, like deep furrows, each the channel of a watercourse, insignificant enough in dry weather, but attaining considerable dimensions during and after rain. Some of these little mountain bays present scenes of great wildness. Along the course of the stream the rock is denuded of its covering of trees, even the soil being swept away; there is an uninterrupted view to the precipices above, and to the dark bed of the Giffre below; and you may look upwards through an interminable vista of rich and variegated foliage, and see a light feathery waterfall dancing gracefully down a grand limestone crag apparently just above your head, while on turning round you catch one glimpse of the foaming torrent of the Giffre, and perhaps hear faintly the roar of its waters hurrying by at a great distance below. In the month of September, when the forests are dyed with the russet hues of autumn, and when the sides of the little ravines are thickly spangled with the large bright blue flowers of the *gentiana ciliata*, nothing can exceed the beauty of some of these ravines.

In one place, a great pine tree stands like a tall beacon by the side of the path, towering in solitary pride to a height of from 100 to 150 feet — its stem as straight as an arrow, broken by not a single branch for the first fifty or sixty feet; in another, a little foot-path leads down one of the steepest of the steep slopes of grass, and following its course with our eyes, we see that the dark gorge, hundreds of feet below us, is spanned by a frail bridge of rough fir poles, affording a wild and gloomy passage into the great forests that clothe the opposite bank. We keep constantly winding somewhat to the left; wherever a break in the wood shows us more of the distant prospect, we see that the precipices of the Buet itself are coming into sight; and at length we emerge from the wood and gain a grassy knoll, whence for the first time we get a view of the head of the valley, and of the beautiful plateau on which the Chalets des Fonds are built. The knoll is itself so pleasantly situated, and the pastures above it are so green and fresh, that one almost wonders to see it crowned by no chalets of its own; but the eye of the practised mountaineer will soon observe that it is in a line with a sort of furrow in the slopes above—that a few chalets used by the peasants to whom the upper pastures belong are carefully placed on the highest part of a ridge by the side of the furrow—and that in the line of the furrow itself every tree and shrub is gone; and he will be at no loss to suspect, what is the fact, that this tempting spot is swept by the avalanches of spring, and that anything erected upon it would assuredly be hurled, before a year had passed, into the torrent of the Giffre.

The lofty wall of limestone on the left now recedes, and in places the slopes of pasture-land reach to such a height as almost to conceal the precipices by which they are everywhere surmounted. The wooded heights on the opposite bank of the Giffre push forward their bases so as to occupy nearly half of the picture, and the contracted valley of the Giffre opens out into a wide amphitheatre of magnificent precipices, bearing aloft at a vast height the glaciers of the Buet. The precipices are loftiest and most abrupt towards the left, in the deepest recess of the horse-shoe; here, however, they are partially concealed by slopes of wood and pasture-land, similar to those already passed; but advancing further towards the centre of the view, and immediately in front of us, is one of those formations which look as if they were meant to give strength and solidity to the gigantic wall of natural masonry above — a great spur of mountain, banked up against the crags of the Buet, and falling away right and left on each side of a definite ridge, till the lateral slopes meet some similar formation, where the line of their junction is marked by the stream that steals down between them. This "buttress of an Alp"— to use Mr. Ruskin's felicitous expression — is partly clad with luxuriant forests, composed in the upper regions of fir-trees only, in the lower, slightly interspersed with beech; but the central ridge, and a large portion of both faces, consist of some of the finest grass-land in the Alps. Indeed, the pasturages of "Les Fonds," as they are called, enjoy a reputation second to none in this district except those of "Les Salles," above the cascade of "La Pleureuse;" and for the purpose of tending the cattle annually brought hither to feed, and of carrying on the operations of the dairy, a village of not less than fifty or sixty chalets has been built on the upper portion of a small plateau not much higher than the knoll on which we stand.

Descending a short distance, and passing beneath the welcome shade of a wood of beautiful beeches, through whose slender foliage the straggling sunbeams dart and play in fitful patterns on the moss-grown bank, we draw rapidly near to the torrent, now but a few yards below us. Presently, emerging from the trees, we come upon a rude bridge across the principal arm of the stream which pours from the left, fed chiefly, as its turbid aspect shows, by the meltings of the glaciers of the Buet. The smaller branch — a comparatively insignificant rivulet, called the Ruisseau des Fonds — descends from the other side of the Montagne des Fonds, and issuing from a dark and romantic gorge a few yards to the right of the bridge, instantly loses its individuality, and sinks into a petty tributary of the Giffre.

Quitting the friendly shelter of the wood, we mount a bare hill-side by short and clumsy zig-zags, and in a very few minutes arrive upon the "Plateau des Fonds." The plateau itself is only a tolerably level piece of pasture-land, some few acres in extent, but surrounded by scenery of no common grandeur. It is placed nearly in the centre of the great amphitheatre of precipices which opened on us at the grassy knoll whence we first caught sight of the chalets; but it is only from this spot that their full extent can be seen, or their magnificence appreciated. They stretch in one long dark and frowning wall from north to south-east of the spectator, attaining their greatest height, and presenting their wildest aspect, about midway between the two extremities of the arc. At its northern end they are crowned by grass-land so steep as to make one wonder that even Alpine sheep and Alpine shepherds dare to trust themselves upon its slippery surface just above those tremendous crags. As the precipices increase in height, however, the strip of verdure diminishes in breadth; and from the middle of the horse-shoe to its south-eastern point, the line of bare rock either stands out sharply against the sky, or is capped by a glistening patch of glacier. In several places the dark surface of the crag is dashed by a streak of white foam, or seen through the waving medium of a thin web of water-drops, swayed to and fro by every passing breath of air.

It is difficult to estimate heights correctly by the eye, still more so to judge of them from recollection, but I think the loftiest portion of this magnificent crescent cannot be less than 2500 or 3000 feet in height. Nor is the south-eastern extremity of the arc of less imposing aspect, though its crags are not on so colossal a scale; for their inferiority in elevation is due, not so much to a lowering of the actual outline of the ridge, as to the height attained by the pastures of Les Fonds, and the rich growth of fir-wood which protects them from the avalanches of April and May. In fact, by climbing to the summit of the pastures, access may be gained to the crags above; they are broken by narrow rifts, cut far into the substance of the mountain by the torrents of spring, and, by their depth of shadow, throw out the intervening masses into a bold relief that makes them look like the outworks and watch-towers of a gigantic fortress. They belong in fact to a kind of for-

VIEW FROM THE ENGANO REST,
looking towards the Pass.

mation which gives a very peculiar and wonderful character to a deep valley opening beyond them, further to the south, by which the ascent of the Buet and the passage of the Col de l'Échaud are made. A small portion of this valley is seen from the Plateau des Fonds, but it is not nearly enough to give an accurate notion of the true character of the scenery; nor is it till a mile or two further along the path towards the Buet that one gets the least idea of the depth and wildness of this great inlet, when, on rounding a projecting spur of the mountain, you come suddenly upon it. The part of the valley visible from the plateau is seen over a great fir forest. It is obviously but the opening to a deeper recess, which the imagination is free to picture as beautiful as it will. Patches of steeply-sloping soil, however, perched among the precipices, and clad with a sturdy growth of shrubs, create a pleasant variety in the prospect; and it is interesting to know that they are still an occasional, if no longer a favourite, haunt of the chamois.

Turning, lastly, to the west, we look down the valley by which we have ascended; the Pointe de Salles is now on our left, though only its loftiest point can be seen soaring above the nearer mountain ranges. As we stand at the edge of the plateau, under the welcome shade of some splendid fir-trees, we see that we are upon a tongue of land, bounded by the converging waters of the Ruisseau des Fonds on the left, and of the Giffre on the right; we look down a steep fir-clad slope, and have the little bridge and the junction of the streams at our feet; and it is pleasant to catch here and there through openings in the woods bright gleams of light reflected from the rushing waters, as the impetuous torrent hurries from the chafing impediments which vex it in its earlier course, to seek the gentler declivities and softer bed awaiting it in the pleasant valleys far below.

Circumstances which I am going to mention have given this wild spot and the very lovely valley leading to it a special interest in my eyes; and while I cannot help acknowledging the possibility that they may have insensibly led me to over-estimate its attractions, they certainly afford the most conclusive proof of the sincerity of my admiration. A portion of the Plateau des Fonds, and of the wild ravines beneath it, belongs to me; and just on the spot which commands the finest view of all, a chalet is fast rising which I can call my own; and though I certainly should not trouble the reader with matters affecting myself only, the circumstances connected with my acquisition of the land were so curious, and threw such a light upon the character of the people and upon some of the most powerful influences then at work in Sardinian politics — this part of Sardinia then had a constitutional and political existence — that I think a short account of them will be found not wanting in interest, though it be but the melancholy interest attaching to the departed life of a once free province.

It was in the month of August, 1857, that I first saw the Plateau des Fonds. I was descending from the summit of the Buet in company with Balmat and an English friend. The scenery struck us as uncommon in character and unique in beauty, and as we stood at the edge of the level ground, it passed through my mind what a glorious site it would be for a chalet. A day or two afterwards we both wished to revisit the spot, for we could neither of us call to mind in our Alpine experiences a view that had pleased us equally. Finding that our second visit did but strengthen our impressions o the rare beauty of the scenery, the passing thought of the former day returned, and began to assume the character of a definite wish. I set to work to make inquiries about the price of land in the neighbourhood, and the ownership of this particular spot. The value of land I found to be moderate enough — about 200 francs per "journal," (or somewhere about 8*l.* an acre,) being esteemed a high price for anything in that vicinity. The land in question, however, I found to be part of an extensive district of pasture-land and forest belonging to the " commune " of Sixt — a division in civil affairs somewhat answering to a parish in ecclesiastical matters—owned in fee simple by the "commune" in general, but subject to rights of pasturage and woodcutting, which might be exercised by every proprietor of land in the commune. This was not an encouraging state of things to deal with; and, had I been aware what would be involved in the undertaking, I should probably have hesitated before making the attempt. The affairs of a commune are managed by councillors elected for a certain term by the persons liable to communal imposts and possessing communal rights. At Sixt the council consisted of fifteen members, including the Syndic and Vice-Syndic, who are a sort of mayor and deputy mayor, elected triennially by the council. The council of a commune, I learned, could sell land belonging to the commune, but the resolutions upon which the sale was to be founded must be passed either at one particular meeting of the council, or at a meeting specially summoned for the purpose by the

Intendant, the chief civil officer of the province. The matter was not ended, however, with the deliberation of the council, but the resolution must receive the sanction of the Intendant, and be confirmed by a sort of judicial inquiry held by the "juge de paix," assisted by experts, in order to ascertain that the council is not parting with the property of the commune at a price below the market value. The whole proceedings had then to be laid before the Minister of the Interior, who might exercise his discretion as to whether they should be ratified or not. It was not until they had received the royal approbation, under the sign-manual, that the sale could be carried out. What the formalities may now be, under the Imperial rule, I cannot tell.

I was obliged to leave Sixt without prosecuting the matter, and was not able to return till the middle of September, when I proceeded at once to sound the communal authorities. I applied, in the first instance, to Monsieur Pasquier, a respected notary of Samoëns, and secretary to the commune of Sixt, by whom I was introduced to the Syndic, the Vice-Syndic, and several of the councillors — all peasants of the district, but numbering amongst them some very intelligent and business-like men. The following day happened to be Sunday, when, after morning mass, the sittings of the council are held, and the Syndic took the opportunity of mentioning my proposal and seeing how it was likely to be received. It was agreed that on the Monday I should go up to Les Fonds with as many of the council as chose to attend, and point out to them exactly what I wished to buy. This was done, and I met some eight or nine of the council on the spot, and pointed out what I should like to acquire, and explained my objects in proposing to purchase. My explanations appeared to give general satisfaction, and we parted excellent friends, every one assuring me that I might command his vote. It was arranged that I should go to Bonneville, and obtain, if possible, the authority of the Intendant for the holding of a special sitting of the council on the Sunday following, and return to Sixt before that day to make my formal proposition for the purchase.

The then Intendant of the Province of Faucigny was the Count d'Elia, who has since been removed to the higher Intendancy of the Province of Salluces, a Piedmontese gentleman of excellent family, and the husband of an accomplished and amiable English lady; a zealous and vigorous administrator, and a man of enlarged and liberal views. It is impossible for me to express too strongly my sense of the courtesy with which a hearing was granted, and the promptitude with which all the assistance that official activity could give was rendered to me. The same day that I called upon the Intendant, I returned to Chamouni, which was then my head-quarters, and before I had reached my destination, the official authority to the Syndic, to hold an extraordinary meeting of the council, was on its way to Sixt.

The following Saturday I repaired again to Sixt, but soon found that an influence had been at work, the strength of which I had been led by Monsieur Pasquier, and others, to undervalue. The curé of Sixt is an ecclesiastic of the old régime, to whom the growing independence and political activity of the people had been as gall and wormwood, and who sighed for the good old days before the Constitution of 1848, when clerical influence predominated in the state, when all discussion of political or ecclesiastical matters was rigidly suppressed, and when men even on the bare mountain-sides or on the trackless glaciers would 'bate their breath and look round them with the caution of habitual suspicion, if they ventured to utter a word of comment on the powers that be, from the King to the Commissary of Police, or from the Archbishop of Turin to the "Vicaire" of the parish. For some years past, before the late "cession" was mooted, the priesthood not only of Savoy, but throughout Sardinia, had occupied a vastly different position, and it is difficult for any one who has not had the opportunity of seeing a little below the surface, to conceive the bitter dislike and rooted suspicion with which the priesthood, as an order, were regarded almost everywhere by the friends of constitutional government and moderate reform throughout the kingdom. All expression of these, or any other political feelings, will now in all probability be effectually put a stop to under the Imperial rule; but at the time I speak of, it appeared that the inveterate jealousy entertained towards the priests was scarcely likely to subside until they were satisfied to confine themselves to their legitimate functions and to abandon their pretensions to political power. It could not be expected that they on their part should succumb without a struggle, and hence arose an actual alienation from the church, or at least from the hierarchy, of a great portion of the intelligence and worth of the Sardinian people. A few months later, namely, in the early part of 1858, this mutual repulsion was carried to a still greater length; for at the several elections which then took place, the priestly party made a desperate effort to recover their lost ground; an effort which signally failed, and resulted both in reducing their influence still lower than it was before, and in embittering the hostility with which they were regarded by those who styled themselves the "friends of progress."

When I began my negotiations, I was guided, naturally enough, by the advice of Monsieur Pasquier and other persons of the "advance" party; who certainly underrated the strength of Monsieur le Curé and his friends. When I proposed to go and see the curé and endeavour to disarm his apprehended opposition, they assured me such a step was needless, and that I need not trouble myself about his power. Sixt, however, is just one of those remote places where the influence of the priesthood was likely to be strongest and most durable; and naturally enough, with his political and social views, the curé did not approve of the proposal of an Englishman, of all people in the world, to come and build himself an habitation, though it were only for an occasional long-vacation sojourn, within his parish. Visions of "a protestant propaganda," and perhaps of French translations of Exeter Hall tracts against the Pope and auricular confession (for Monsieur le Curé is a gentleman of learning and education, and well acquainted with what is passing in the world beyond his valley) started up before his eyes, and he resolved that the foreign intruder should not come to be a thorn in his side if he could help it. Accordingly, I found on my return to Sixt that no stone had been left unturned to get a majority in the council to take the high conservative view of the question. There would be a protestant crusade in the valley; domestic purity would suffer even more severely than religious orthodoxy; one intruder would give rise to another, and their "montagnes" (sufficient for many times the number of cattle at present pastured upon them), would be cut up into building patches to satisfy the vagaries of English taste; then the cattle and goats would stray over the land of this English aristocrat, who would impound them and refuse to release them except upon payment of exorbitant compensation; besides it was all nonsense about his wanting to build a place for autumn recreation; would he be likely to come a thousand miles from home for such a purpose? The fact was, he had found the vein of gold ore Jaques Balmat had failed to discover; and their forests — the pride and wealth of the valley —

would be destroyed to find fuel for his smelting furnaces — or if not that, he wanted to build an hotel, or some similar abomination; and why should they be condemned to have their valley overrun by foreigners, like that of Chamouni?

I cannot say of my own knowledge, of course, that all these remarkable objections emanated from the curé; I only know that I have been assured they did over and over again both by friends and opponents, and that that gentleman himself did not disclaim having taken a very active part against me, when, after the matter was all settled, I wrote to him and called upon him to express the hope that we should not be the worse friends for having taken different views on a subject in which both were interested. But from whatever quarter they came, I found they had quite altered the aspect of things in the five days between my two visits. The arguments which seemed to have the greatest weight were, naturally enough, those which were most palpably absurd. The gold mine was a great stumbling-block, and the destruction of forests in the valley of the Bas Giffre, where the iron works had been carried on, was triumphantly appealed to as a fair measure of the apprehended calamity. Then, my modest request to be allowed to pasture a single cow for six weeks on the vast feeding grounds of the commune was made great use of against me. It would "gêner leur montagne," just as, by my arbitrary and oppressive proceedings in respect of strayed cattle, I should enrich myself at the expense of my poor neighbours. Incredible as it may seem, even the hotel argument was gravely urged and seriously discussed. Eventually, it appeared that there would be six in favour of my proposition and seven against it, if it went to the vote, but that some of the majority would not object to grant me a lease for thirty years upon certain very stringent conditions.

I considered the business at an end, but asked Monsieur Pasquier to give me a copy of the *procès-verbal* — the minutes of the meeting — which consisted of a very faithful abstract of the general discussion, drawn up by himself and signed by the Syndic and some of the councillors; and on the following day I went to Bonneville, on my way home to England, where I called on the Count d'Elia and showed it to him. He pointed out to me that, no vote having been actually taken, the question was still open, and begged me not to let the matter rest, but to execute a power of attorney in favour of some person in whom I had confidence, and to leave all the rest to him, assuring me that my interests should be attended to — an assurance more than carried out by him, as the sequel will show. So handsome an offer could only be gratefully accepted; I gave Balmat a power of attorney to act for me, and then returned to England. Count d'Elia thought it the more prudent course to let the matter sleep until the strong feeling excited by the recent debate had somewhat evaporated; but towards the close of the autumn he not only convoked another extraordinary meeting of the council, but took the trouble to go himself from Bonneville to Sixt — four or five hours' journey — in order to be present at the deliberation, and to assist the council by his advice, as he was by law entitled, should he think fit, to do. The sitting was a long and stormy one. Fourteen out of the fifteen councillors were present; and so high did party feeling run, that both the Intendant and Monsieur Pasquier were grossly insulted by two of the recalcitrant members. At length a vote was taken, when the numbers were exactly equal — seven and seven — the Intendant having the right to be present and to join in the discussion, but not to vote. Count d'Elia then turned to the article of the law applicable to such a case, and in conformity with it called upon the Syndic to give his casting vote. The Syndic had all along been one of my most zealous friends, believing with the Intendant that anything which could tend to open the valley of Sixt to strangers, and to bring the population in contact with the rest of the world, would be greatly to the interest of the district. The resolution to sell the land was, therefore, carried by the casting vote of the chairman. I was assured by every one that nothing but the great tact and temper of the Intendant could have brought about this result. Curiously enough, the vote had scarcely been taken, when the fifteenth councillor, who was a furious opponent of the project, walked in and claimed to vote; but it was too late, the resolution was already carried and the vote recorded. I have always accused Balmat or some other of my zealous friends of having contrived that his boots should be mislaid that morning; but they do not confess to any such manœuvre.

It might be supposed that the substantial part of the business was now accomplished, and that the rest would be mere matter of form; but it was no such thing. Beaten in the council, the opposition betook themselves to memorialising the Minister of the Interior against the authorisation of the sale.

Petitions were hawked about the commune of Sixt and the neighbouring commune of Samoëns; and even from Paris, whither a great number of the young men of this valley constantly resort to exercise their vocations as stone-masons, carpenters, and waiters, sheets upon sheets of signatures were forwarded to Turin protesting against the measure. Some persons of considerable political influence were induced also to bestir themselves; and the Minister hesitated long which way to decide. By this time, however, the whole of the neighbouring districts had taken up the question as a case of progress or retrogression, and very active influence was used by gentlemen of Samoëns and the neighbourhood, to whom I was personally a complete stranger, but who considered it of great importance that the priestly view of the question should not prevail. Fortunately for me, just at this time my kind friend the Count d'Elia was promoted to the Intendancy of Salluces, not far from Turin; and when he went up to the capital on receiving this appointment, he took care that the Minister should be fully possessed of *his* views: and at length, in the spring of 1858, the requisite authorisation was signed by the king, and nothing remained but to take the formal steps necessary to complete the purchase. Here, however, difficulties again presented themselves. The delegates named by the council to execute the conveyance refused to have anything to do with it, and at one time I was afraid I should have to proceed against them by a kind of *mandamus:* however, after a great deal of trouble, which I am sorry to say fell heavily upon my friends rather than upon myself, the difficulty was got over by another exercise of the royal prerogative in the nomination of the new Intendant of the province, Monsieur Felix de Bergöens, as the representative of the commune for the purpose of executing the act of sale. In consequence of all these delays, it was not till the month of July, 1858, that the conveyance was actually executed. Of course, under the circumstances, I paid more for the land than it was worth. Guided by the advice of the Count d'Elia, I offered more than twice its market value, or about 16*l.* per "journal;" had I not done so, I should never have had it at all. It was curious to see that the jealousy of my pounding the cattle continued to the last; for in the conveyance it is stipulated, not only that I shall properly enclose my purchase, but that I shall not seize any cattle or goats that may stray thereupon.

An English lawyer reading this account would, I

think, see in it the elements of a pretty heavy solicitor's bill. He will be as much surprised as I was, to learn that beyond the ordinary expenses of conveyance, stamps, fees, and the like, which are not light in Sardinia, the whole affair did not cost me 20*l*., nor anything like it. The expenses would no doubt have been much greater had I not from first to last been backed with a thorough goodwill by every official personage. There was, at that time, an incredible amount of "circumlocution" in Sardinia: the formalities to be gone through in dealing with any sort of public right were absolutely endless, and had there been the least unwillingness on the part of the authorities to help me, my project would inevitably have been smothered in the slough of despond of official routine. But whatever may be the faults of the administrative system, Sardinia — or what is left of her — is happy indeed if her high public servants in general are like the only two with whom I have had to deal, both of whom I have found accessible at all times, prompt and vigorous in action, free from official mystery and reserve in speech, and full of wise and liberal views on social and political questions. Of my obligations to the Count d'Elia, and my high estimate of his character and qualities, I have already spoken. His successor, Monsieur de Bergöens, is one of the most enlightened men I have the pleasure of knowing; and as an administrative officer, I believe he has few equals. The promptitude and regularity with which business was despatched in his office, were something extraordinary; and no one, I believe, can be found who has ever had occasion to approach him in his official capacity who is not loud in his praises of his courtesy, frankness, and accessibility. Travellers who visited Chamouni last autumn, and who were familiar with it in previous years, found out the difference to their comfort and convenience, as well as to their purses, effected by the recent alterations in the odious regulations as to guides, which had been so long felt as an intolerable annoyance: it is right they should know that it is in no small degree to the energy, patience, and perseverance of Monsieur de Bergöens that they owe the improvement that has taken place.

I fear this narrative has already grown long enough; but I must add a few words as to some subsequent occurrences, because they illustrate a trait of the national character exceedingly creditable to the people, and which at the time it was impossible to help looking upon as most hopeful for the future prospects of constitutional government in Sardinia, as far at least as the Savoyards were concerned.

I went abroad again in the autumn of 1858, and Sixt was naturally the first place I was anxious to visit. I wrote to Balmat to meet me at Sixt on the 15th of August, but took no other steps to announce my arrival. Indeed, knowing the dissensions to which my proposal had given rise, I felt inclined rather to sneak in unobserved than to proclaim my coming beforehand. We reached Samoëns, about two hours' walk from Sixt, between three and four o'clock in the afternoon of the 15th of August; and as my friends were not less struck than I had formerly been with the beauty of the place, we determined to sleep there and go on the next morning. Before dinner could be served, I was told that a deputation from Sixt wished to see me; and I found three or four of the councilmen waiting to assure me, in the name of the commune, that a hearty welcome would be given to us by all parties, and that I need not fear the slightest unpleasantness in consequence of what had taken place. The most resolute of my antagonists, they said, had opposed me on public grounds, and because they thought it would be better for the valley that I should not establish myself there; but now the matter was once decided, their only wish was to receive us as friends, and to offer us every facility for carrying on our operations. They had come from Sixt to seek me, and to offer to my wife and myself the expression of their goodwill. Such assurances were very pleasant, and afforded no little relief to my wife, who did not much fancy settling amongst a population to whom we might be objects of dislike.

This was not all, however; that evening, to our great surprise, as we sat in the balcony, we were serenaded by an excellent band, composed of pretty nearly all the gentry of Samoëns and the neighbourhood. My friend, Monsieur Pasquier, played the trombone, and the brother of the Syndic of Samoëns — one of the wealthiest proprietors of the district — was the leader. I found, upon my thanking these gentlemen for the honour they did us, that our arrival was viewed as a matter of deep interest, inasmuch as it marked the triumph of liberal views over exclusive and antiquated prejudices. The serenade was followed by a salute of cannon, and by a very pretty display of fireworks.

The next morning we found that our friends from Sixt had quite correctly represented the feeling of the people towards us. We were met half-way from Samoëns by a deputation consisting indifferently of supporters and opponents, and welcomed again, as we crossed the boundary of the commune, in the most kind and gratifying manner, while the rocks at the curious passage of Les Tines rang and rang again with the grand echoes of another salute. Similar honours awaited us as we passed through the market-place at Sixt, and an excellent lunch was provided for us by our hospitable friends.

Nor was all this display mere show and talk. The spirit from which it proceeded was exemplified in every transaction I had with the council. I had many requests to make for wood and stone, and sand, for the concession of the right to set up a saw-mill and a lime-kiln; and had I had any sort of opposition to encounter, I should have found the autumn far too short to carry out the necessary arrangements for beginning to build in the following spring. But not a murmur was raised against me, and former friends and former opponents vied with one another as to which could serve me most effectually. I have already intimated that the official formalities to be gone through in Sardinia when any sort of public right is concerned, are something almost beyond belief, and I should very much doubt if business of the like kind was ever before, in Sardinia, carried successfully through all the necessary steps in so short time. From the communal and from the provincial authorities alike, I received nothing but the promptest attention and the most hearty support. Wherever we went we were met with smiling faces, and assurances that the people were glad to see us. It is true these words of welcome were often spoken in a patois very difficult to understand — but it was impossible to mistake their import or to doubt their sincerity. We should certainly have been killed had we drunk one quarter of the excellent milk that was offered us whenever we approached a chalet where cows were kept. We were at Sixt twice during the autumn, for several days each time, constantly visiting Les Fonds, and in constant intercourse with the population, and it is difficult to convey an adequate idea of the pleasant way in which we were uniformly greeted and treated by every one.

Considering the angry feelings which had been excited about this matter, it must be allowed that the behaviour of the defeated minority did them great credit; it seemed to me to indicate an aptitude for constitutional government and free institutions that one fondly hoped might augur well for the prosperity of Sardinia. These peasants of Sixt appear to me to have fathomed the great secret of all constitutional government, and to have learned to recognise the duty of the minority to yield to the majority. "We had our own views of what was right," my former opponents said to me over and over again, "and while it was an open question, we resisted your proposition with all our might, and in every way the law allowed us. But it is decided now; we have said our say, and given our votes; we have been fairly beaten, and we do not wish either to complain of the result, or to struggle against the majority by opposing your requests for anything necessary to the full enjoyment of your property. We are now fellow-members of the same commune, and as such have the same interests."

Surely, people who have learned to think, and speak, and act thus, have evinced a capacity for liberty and self-government which is very extraordinary in a nation so recently emancipated from arbitrary power. I was inclined at first to attribute this circumstance to their communal institutions; but I found on inquiry that the character of these was altogether different before 1848; and that under the old régime the communal council—instead of being a representative body, fairly and freely elected by the votes of the inhabitants, independent of government influence or control, enjoying absolute liberty of speech, subject to no kind of external interference, and having the administration of the communal affairs entirely in its own hands—was merely a board nominated by the government, possessing little liberty of speech or action, and having, in fact, nothing in common with the present communal administration but a name. That the communal councils were, at the time I speak of, practically, as well as theoretically, free from government interference or influence, is shown by the incident above mentioned, of the two indignant councilmen offering a gross insult to the Intendant of their province.

The reader must have had, once in his life, a hobby of his own, to be able to understand the full extent of the pleasure given to my wife and myself by the possession of the charming little spot I have endeavoured to describe. All beautiful scenery gains wonderfully by familiarity with its details, and the valley of Sixt seemed to us ever full of new charms each time we passed up it or down it. The last time we repaired thither was three or four days after my ascent of Monte Rosa, recorded in the last chapter of this volume. We approached it from the valley of the Rhone by the Val d'Illiez, passing a night at Champéry on our way. We arrived at

Champéry as late as nine o'clock in the evening. We were wonderfully impressed with that moonlight ride from St. Maurice, but were hardly prepared for the exquisite scene that broke upon us with the morning light. We had been long amongst the wildest and sternest scenery of the Alps, and two days before had made the passage of the Diablerets in weather which seemed in good keeping with the name, and all these circumstances combined by their contrast to quicken our sense of the rich and luxuriant beauties of Champéry. The valley appeared to us, for the moment, the loveliest in creation, and we began to think, if not to say, " Oh that we had seen this first!" On inquiry we found the price of land so prodigious that any purchase there would have been hopelessly beyond our means, and we laid that consolation to our hearts. The next day we were at Sixt again, and took our favourite excursion; we were perfectly set at rest—Champéry was not to compare with Les Fonds, and we were still able to pronounce our little plateau the most beautiful spot we knew.

Of course we sought a pleasant name for it, and we wished to find, as most appropriate, some musical term in patois which should bear a characteristic meaning; but the patois of Sixt is not musical, whatever other recommendations it may boast, and, after much deliberation, almost the first name we had thought of seemed the best, and we formally designated it "The Eagle's Nest." I have measured its height above Sixt several times, both by the barometer and by the boiling-water apparatus, and I find it to be in round numbers about 1950 feet above Sixt; and as I estimate Sixt at about 2350 feet above the level of the sea, this gives a height of 4300 for our eyrie — nearly the height of the top of Ben Nevis.

While we were at Chamouni, in 1858, we agreed with a very worthy contractor of Sallenches, M. Grange, who has erected most of the principal buildings at Chamouni, for the construction of our chalet; but we resolved that, if possible, the place should be from first to last our own hobby, and our only architect has been my wife. The very details of the building, the number of steps in the staircases, the arrangement of windows, doors, chimneys, and galleries, are all hers. The lines which I have adopted for the motto of this volume, and which are intended to be carved, after the Swiss fashion, along the base of the galleries, were written by her. M. Grange pronounced that her scale-drawings did not require correction, but would do to work from; and I pre-

I have spoken of the kindness shown
the people of the valley. The heartiness

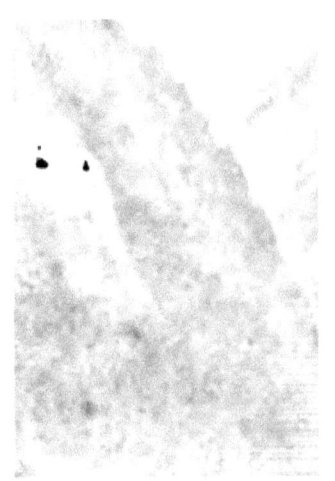

sume, therefore, the original plans have been faithfully carried out. I was not able to go thither in 1859, and therefore have been obliged to trust implicitly, as I may safely do, to M. Grange and Balmat. We were last there on the 29th September, 1858, and on that day we planted with our own hands the stakes which were intended to mark out the limits of the building, and the situations of the principal doors and windows. I remember well each of us standing in turn, supported by the other, on the ends of some of our newly-planted posts, to raise ourselves to the level of the ground floor, and see exactly what would be the views from each of the sitting-rooms. Balmat and I then laid out a beautiful winding path, to lead from the bridge over the Giffre through our own little property up to the chalet, and with some difficulty I got my wife down by the projected route, and was glad to find that it pleased her taste as much as my own. As we left the plateau, avowedly for the last time that season, she said to me, "I wonder whether we shall ever be here together again!"—words destined, alas! to find a mournful echo in the commands of Providence.

I have spoken of the kindness shown to us by the people of the valley. The heartiness with which we were greeted by our neighbours between Sixt and Les Fonds, whenever we appeared amongst them, was delightful. One day we had gone up to within half an hour's walk of the Eagle's Nest, and were sketching and photographing the fine view of the plateau and the crags of the Buet behind it, when a peasant girl passed, coming from Les Fonds, picking hemp (pulling off, that is, the outside covering of the stalks) as she went along. We had not intended to go farther on that occasion, as there were a great number of people at work at the Chalets des Fonds, spreading manure over the ground, preparatory to leaving for the lower pastures, which they were about to do the next day. We learned from the girl, however, that we had been seen, and were anxiously expected by the good people above, and that it would cause great disappointment if we did not make our appearance. We thought, as this was the case, we had better go on; so when we had dined, we left the photographic apparatus where it was, and pursued our way to the Eagle's Nest. After visiting our own ground, we went on to the chalets, where we found a large crowd waiting to welcome us. We were soon overpowered with offers of milk, and thinking it would please the good folks, we went with one woman to her chalet to get some. The spaces or little streets between the rows of chalets are none of the cleanest, but we managed to pick our way to the door where the woman was waiting for us, and stooping, as was necessary, entered the chalet. It was almost dark, but the good woman went into a still darker inner room to get the milk, handing my wife a stool to sit upon. The only other articles in the room besides the stool, were a half-filled sack lying against the wall, and a large long-legged pig, very much at his ease, for he stalked about with a lordly air, and poked his long nose into every hole and corner. Presently my wife heard a little tinkle behind her, and looking round found a little calf rubbing its nose against her mantle, from behind a railing by which it was kept to its own portion of the room. Presently the woman came out from the inner sanctum with a small washing-tub half full of milk, which she offered to me to drink from, while she handed my wife some in a thick red earthenware cup. After we had drunk as much as we could and thanked our worthy hostess, we went into another chalet, where I had found what I thought would interest my wife, a baby packed up in a cradle, where it remained all day without moving hand or foot. It was eight months old, and seemed to me a model baby, for it was perfectly contented and never uttered a sound. There was soon a concourse of women in the chalet when they saw we stayed to look at the baby, and they all jabbered patois as fast as they could, and were extremely amused when we could not understand all they said. After shaking hands with them all round, we parted the best friends in the world.

There is a curious similarity amongst nearly all the young women. The old ones are plain enough, but many of the young ones are pleasing; all with rather flat faces and large features, but with a pleasant, good-tempered expression and bright eyes. It often happened that we could hardly tell the difference between one and another. They generally go about with bare feet, and if they feel it a duty they owe to society to put on shoes on special occasions, get rid of them as soon as they can. We frequently used to meet them going barefoot up the steep hills, carrying a considerable weight in a basket balanced on their heads, and stripping the hemp as they went along. Nearly all the women, and many of the men and all the children, were dressed in a dark blue woollen home-spun stuff; the little children wear a dark close-fitting cap — almost a skull-cap; even the little baby in the cradle had one.

Both men and women seemed proud of their pretty valley, for nearly all of them asked us if we did not find it "ben brave" — very pretty. The out-of-door life and the hard work they are accustomed to age them rapidly, and accordingly they were very much surprised at our young looks. They pronounced me to be about nineteen and my wife still younger, and could hardly be brought to believe that we had been married more than four years and had a couple of children at home. Large families seemed to us to be the rule. I remember one day passing a woman on our way home to Sixt, standing at the door of her chalet, rising out of the midst of a cluster of eight or ten small children; and apparently with any number more in the background. She stopped us to ask the usual questions — how old we were, and how many children we had. She did not seem at all satisfied with our modest allowance, whereupon Balmat, who had a joke for everybody, complimented her upon her own fine family. She laughed, and offered to make him a present of six. He immediately began fumbling in his pockets, and said, " Well, I have room here for three or four," whereupon the whole bevy vanished into the chalet in a paroxysm of fright.

CHAP. V.

> "He listened and looked up. I looked up too;
> And twice there came a hiss that thro' me thrilled!
> 'Twas heard no more. A chamois on the cliff
> Had roused his fellows with that cry of fear,
> And all were gone."—ROGERS.

THE BUET.

ASCENT FROM CHAMOUNI. — THE CASCADE BÉRARD. — THE "PIERRE BÉRARD."—ROUGH QUARTERS. — AN UNEXPECTED MEETING. — HOW WE PASSED THE NIGHT AND HOW THE GUIDES PASSED THE NIGHT.— DEEP STRIE. — DAYBREAK ON MONT BLANC. — THE SUMMIT. — SEA OF CLOUDS.—DESCENT TO SIXT.—A WONDERFUL AMPHITHEATRE.— THE CHAMOIS.—FIRST IMPRESSIONS OF THE PLATEAU DES FONDS.— ASCENT FROM SIXT.—VIEW FROM THE COL DE L'ÉCHAUD.—SEVERE ATTACK OF ILLNESS. — A DILEMMA. — FORWARD ! — THE DISTANT CATTLE BELLS. — DEEP SNOW. — THE CHALET BÉRARD REACHED. — A CLOSE BARGAIN.—A SIMPLE CURE.

IT was on the 16th of August 1857 that I started for my first trip to the Buet. I had arrived some days before from England, tired and jaded, and was disappointed to find that vigour of body and elasticity of mind did not seem to return so rapidly as I have generally found to be the case under the influence of the pure air of the glaciers. I have sometimes noticed that there is nothing like a "grande course" for "setting up," as the doctors would call it, the restorative processes; but neither my friend W. nor myself felt very much disposed for one of the first magnitude — so we agreed to try the Buet as a sort of happy medium between the smaller and the really great excursions. A second excellent friend, R., with whom I crossed the Glaciers du Tour and de Salena, and ascended Mont Blanc, a few days later, was unable to leave the house owing to the reappearance of an old strain to the knee; so we left him to the hospitable care of Madame Ferdinand, at the Hôtel Royal, and started off a little after mid-day, accompanied by Balmat and François Cachat. We took the familiar track of the Tête Noire till we arrived just below the highest part of the pass, and there struck across to the left, passing amongst a vast accumulation of polished blocks, which showed how low the glaciers of the Aiguilles Rouges and the Buet had once descended. At this point you have just reached the easternmost extremity of the chain of the Aiguilles Rouges, which you must round; for the valley that separates it from the system of the Buet lies at the back of the chain, as looked at from Argentières. Indeed, it is not till you are nearly or quite at the highest part of the Tête Noire that you become aware of its existence; till then the lofty black crags which form the northern barrier of the Val Orsine appear almost to join on to the system of the Aiguilles Rouges. In ascending the Val Orsine, as when coming from Martigny, the true state of the case is easy enough to discern, and a deep indentation is seen to separate the Aiguilles Rouges from the group of the Buet.

At the entrance to this valley is situated one of the finest waterfalls in this part of the Alps — the Cascade Bérard. It seems to me a pity for any traveller passing along the Tête Noire in either direction, to neglect the half hour or hour's détour which is needed to visit this picturesque and beautiful scene. When I first saw it, on our way to the Buet, we were enveloped in a thick drizzling rain, which prevented our seeing many hundred yards in any direction: notwithstanding this disadvantage, the Cascade Bérard appeared to me even then to present such a scene of wildness and beauty combined as I had scarcely ever seen equalled. Rough boulders of the largest size and of every shape have fallen from the heights above and accumulated in the wildest disorder about the bed of the torrent.

... it is not till you are
... highest part of the Tête Noire
... of its existence; till then the
... which form the northern barrier
... appear almost to join on to the
... Aiguilles Rouges. In ascending the
... coming from Martigny the
... is easy enough to discern, and
... seen to separate the Aiguilles
Rouges from the group of the Buet.

At the entrance to this valley is situated one of
the finest waterfalls in this part of the Alps — the
Cascade Bérard. It seems to me a pity for any
one passing along the Tête Noire in either
... the half hour or hour's détour
... the picturesque and beau-
... I first saw it, on our way to the
B... enveloped in a thick drizzling rain,
which prevented our seeing many hundred yards in
any direction, notwithstanding this disadvantage,
the Cascade Bérard appeared to me even then to pre-
a... ...uness and beauty combined
... ever seen equalled. Rocks
... ...d of every shape I we
full... ...es and accumulated in
the ...est disorder ... the bed of the torrent

They are covered with a soft tapestry of green moss, and from among them, out of clefts filled up with the débris of centuries, spring audacious mountain firs, crowning the tops of inaccessible precipices or nestled among groups of rugged crags. A considerable volume of water thunders over a huge projecting roof of limestone before taking its bold plunge of two or three hundred feet, and leaves a wild passage behind its little amphitheatre of water. In other places the fallen rocks have left deep caverns and grottoes, where you need artificial light to grope your way. In short, for one who cares for the detailed and individual beauties of nature as well as for the more comprehensive attractions of a grand prospect, it is a very delightful and interesting scene. I was glad to find, when passing through the Tête Noire again in 1858, that my impressions were confirmed by a second visit, and that my admiration of the cascade was fully shared by my wife, who was then my companion. We had slept at one of the inns on the Tête Noire, on purpose to have a long day before us to sketch and photograph in this exquisite valley — the "sketcher's paradise," as it appeared to my companion — and we spent several hours most pleasantly, within two or three hundred yards of the cascade.

At the waterfall the torrent was crossed, and after a short halt at a chalet where some little refreshment may be had, W. and I continued our route. We wound our way up a somewhat rugged path under the precipices of the Buet system, sometimes over tolerably open slopes of grass, sometimes amongst scattered fir-woods, till we reached an alluvial plain of some extent, where the inclination is very slight. The great beauty of the entrance to this valley seems to hold out the promise of an interesting walk; but it is a most deceptive invitation, for the valley is deep, savage, and monotonous, and the vegetation poor and scanty. For two or three miles we picked our way over the stony bed of the winter's torrent before we arrived at the foot of the actual ascent. The weather had cleared slightly, and we saw the glaciers of the Aiguilles Rouges on the right, of the Buet on the left, and those which cover the connecting ridge that lay in front of us, cradled on their beds of crag, and stretching down towards us as if to invite us onward. A quarter of an hour's climb up a steep and stony " Alp " brought us to the Chalet Bérard, a little structure of which half was ready built by the hand of nature, there being a " Pierre Bérard," under which formerly travellers and shepherds used

THE CHALET BÉRARD.

occasionally to pass the night. A very small amount of labour and skill has turned this natural shelter into a chalet, consisting of a rock kitchen and larder, and two added rooms, each furnished with a bed, and one with a stove also. Above these was a sort of loft, which, when I went up a ladder to look at it, appeared full of wet bedsteads, sodden bedding, and a miscellaneous collection of household articles of one sort or another, all in a more or less advanced stage of damp and discomfort. This was our halting-place for the night.

In coming up from the cascade, I had been walking first, and had, of course, given the pace to the party. I was very conscious of being out of condition, and was tired, out of breath, and palpitating painfully, when, near the top of the last rise, I exclaimed to Balmat with some disappointment that I had no longer the strength I used to have, and that I was afraid my " grandes courses " were almost over. " Oh but," he answered, "at what a pace you have come; we usually reckon two good hours from the Cascade to the Chalet, and you have led us up in an hour and a quarter; Cachat and I are bathed in perspiration." Balmat's remark at once surprised and comforted me, for I had the impression that I had been going slowly. I suppose it was the combination of the sense of feebleness and the fear of hindering my companions that had driven me on.

We had brought up with us some mutton, some bread, and some champagne; so we did pretty well, notwithstanding the drizzling rain that blocked out all ulterior prospects, and gave us very poor hopes for the morrow. We had hardly eaten our meal when the mist lifted for a moment, and disclosed, to our horror, four other travellers struggling up to the same refuge as ourselves. Considering that a week often passes without any one sleeping here besides a resident boy and girl, it was unlucky enough that this party should have chosen the same wet day as ourselves to begin their ascent. W. and I thought "first come, first served," was fairly applicable, and as we fancied the inner room was the more weather-tight of the two, we appropriated it, and placed upon the bed all the marks of possession we could. We had hardly arranged our traps in accordance with this view of the case before in burst three jolly Englishmen, as straight-forward and good-tempered fellows as one might chance to meet in a summer's wanderings, by whom our presence was as unexpected as their arrival had been by us; and we all burst into a hearty laugh at the rencontre, and at our mutual disappointment in finding that neither set could have the place to themselves.

W. and I betook ourselves about eight o'clock to our one small bed, and half undressing, lay down between the sheets. Generally speaking, if there be a flea within a mile he finds me out and is most assiduous in his attentions; yet on this occasion, oddly enough, though I learned that most of the other men were groaning, grumbling, and hunting all the night long, I fell asleep at once and slept tranquilly till past one o'clock, and was hardly touched. A fire had been lighted in the stove, and I was in the hottest place in the hottest room, which became at length almost unbearable. I suppose it became too warm even for the industrious insects in question. Howbeit, at half-past one we all turned out. I had hung my flannel shirt on a nail; some one had hung a macintosh on another nail close by it, and in the morning I was obliged actually to wring my shirt out; a fact which shows what a soaking evening it had been.

I went forth at once into the keen frosty air, and, stumbling over the rocks and boulders which were strewn about the steep side of the mountain, found the cold stream, whose brawling waters guided my ear to their stony bed; it was almost pitch dark, though the rain and mist were all gone, and the stars were shining brightly enough. An *al fresco* bath in such a temperature requires some determination, but has a wonderfully freshening effect, and I returned to the hut quite ready for the early breakfast they were preparing for us. I had the curiosity to inquire how the guides had fared. I could never ascertain the exact truth, but there appeared to be in the loft one bed—and I am sure, from what I saw, it must have been a wet one,—available for the young lady of the chalet, her brother, our two guides, and the two whom our unexpected companions had brought with them; and, as far as I could make out, they passed the night sacré-ing and " faisant la chasse." These little discomforts, however, never seem to interfere with the peace of mind of the guides; and, to judge by the peals of laughter we heard, they must have had almost as cheery a breakfast as we had.

By a quarter to three we were all ready, and began what seemed in the dark a difficult and toilsome ascent up some steep and stony ravines, till we reached the end of the turf, or attempt at turf, and arrived at a system of rocks which do not belong to Buet itself, but form the link between it and the

Aiguilles Rouges. These rocks are interesting to the glacialist, as affording instances of remarkably deep striation. By the imperfect light in which the still distant dawn was already heralding its approach, I could see some striæ full half an inch deep. It is not often that one sees them much more than half that depth. It was too cold, however, to linger for striations or anything else; the temperature was far below freezing, and the thousand points of light that glittered out of the black vault of heaven shone with a blanched and frosty lustre that made us feel almost the colder for looking at them. Everything promised well for the coming day, and the white head of the Buet showing dimly through the darkness, seemed to be but a stone's-throw distant, and to beckon us forward. We cheerfully obeyed the call; and turning to the right as soon as we reached the rocks, made our way over several beds of recent snow, crisp with the frost, and across some couloirs filled with great blocks of stone, on which yesterday's rain had spread a covering of ice. These passed, we gained at length the glacier which connects the Buet itself with the rocks on which we stood. We gladly left the slippery surfaces of crag for the pleasanter footing of the snow-clad glacier, and for about twenty minutes climbed straight up a steep and uniform curtain of ice; then turning again to the right, so as to be working back somewhat in the direction of the Val Orsine, we began a rapid and laborious ascent up a series of craggy spurs and ridges, which lead nearly to the very summit of the Buet.

The day was now approaching rapidly, and distant objects began to stand out clear and sharp against the cold sky. Just as we took to the rocks, Mont Blanc, who must have been silently stealing above the horizon for some little time past, burst suddenly upon our sight, overtopping the Aiguilles Rouges, and presented a sight of almost unparalleled magnificence, looking far higher than he does from Chamouni, cold and marble in the dawning light, and shedding from his hoary top vast rays of ice down into the depths of the valley. I have seen no other view of Mont Blanc which has impressed me with such an idea of his height, his steepness, and his colossal size. We were then meditating the ascent, and I confess to a feeling of something like dismay when I gazed upon him from this spot. It seemed a boundless presumption to fancy that such creatures as we could ever scale that stupendous structure, or resist the searching intensity of the cold which we could see was reigning in that upper world. But soon one kindling ray lighted on the lonely peak, and a brightness as of hope stole over his stern and massive brow. I have often recalled the sight in memory since, and thought how beautiful a parallel seems sometimes to connect the phenomena of the material and the facts of the mental world; as I have noticed and felt how the heart which pierces deepest into the cold atmosphere of sorrow is often the first to catch the sunbeams of fresh and living hope.

Beyond the range of Mont Blanc rose solitary peaks of the Alps of Dauphiné, the highest points alone overtopping the banks of clouds which nestled at their bases; and far, far away in the south-west sprung up to a startling height some great glacier-clad summits which we could not identify. The guides would have it that they belonged to the Pyrenees, but I doubt very much the possibility of their being seen from so great a distance. On our right, as we wound up the greater part of the ascent, was a surging sea of troubled mist, torn into rags by the keen north wind, and tinged with a delicate amber light. The grassy ranges of the Col de Balme rose from the ocean of clouds, and above these towered a huge rampart of Aiguilles, forming one long frowning line of mingled precipice and glacier up to the Monts Maudits and Mont Blanc himself. Further to the east came the Vélan, with his massive system of glaciers; and further still, three isolated peaks alone emerged from the clouds, the Weisshorn, the Matterhorn, and Monte Rosa. Turning yet further to the left, and right in front of us when we addressed ourselves straight to the ascent, came the mass of the Buet himself; and sweeping the eye northward, clear of his great shoulder, we gazed upon the rich pastures of the lower and less snowy Alps between us and the Lake of Geneva,—a pleasing contrast to the sublime desolation of the Aiguilles Rouges, the Mont Blanc, and the Buet. One or two long lines of solemn mist, that lay like marble lakes between the heights towards the Lake of Geneva, marked the course of the valley of the Dranse and its tributary the Val d'Abondance. In the dim distance to the north, the Jura closed the view.

The snow lay deep upon the rocks and upon the ice. The night's frost had formed a hard crust which broke beneath the foot, and, after affording a momentary support, let us plunge suddenly in about six or eight inches at every step. The leading guide found it hard work. I know I was very nearly knocked up with only a quarter of an hour's experience of the task of making the steps, when we reached the summit; Cachat having dropped back exhausted, and I being anxious to see what it was like. The cold was intense. A keen and searching blast from the north froze the snow on our boots—which, unluckily, were not dry after the last night's wetting,—and I, for one, was more near getting my feet frozen than was at all agreeable. It was necessary to keep working the toes about at every step, in order to sustain the circulation at all. At the top of the rocky spurs we stopped for a moment under the best shelter we could find, and had a draught of brandy all round. I dare say I drank a wine-glassful neat—a most nauseous administration, to my taste, but quite necessary.

We then took once more to the snow, and mounting for some time by a gentle and uniform slope, found ourselves at length with no more worlds to conquer, on the brink of a curtain of glacier, which fell away suddenly from beneath our feet. I advanced as near to the edge as I dared, till my stick went through an overhanging cornice of snow, and beneath me I saw a slope, not unlike that at the top of the Wetterhorn, but ending, some two hundred feet below, in a sort of gully between two towers of black crag. Beyond them I could see nothing but a seething cauldron of mist. The view from the summit was little varied from what it had been for some time past, except that in place of the snows of the Buet, we had before us a fresh sea of whirling clouds, which was continually presenting us with some new and fantastic effect, as it was rent and tattered by the nipping wind, and its fragments dashed with one bright rainbow hue after another as they caught and reflected, or refracted, at ever-varying angles, the almost level sunlight. It was but half-past five, so that we had made good speed, and had arrived in ample time to see the early morning view in all its clearness and perfection had the weather favoured us. Still, these effects of mist have beauties of their own, and beauties well worth the labour of the climb, and whenever we turned towards Mont Blanc we could exchange the mysterious phantoms of the shifting clouds for the solemn and stern realities of the changeless mountains and the eternal snows. If you really wish to appreciate the grandeur of Mont Blanc, and to bring home to your mind the scale on which his fabric is reared, go to the summit of the Buet. It is, to my mind, a far more imposing view than even the wonderful scene enjoyed from the Bréven or the Flégère.

The restoring effect of the glacier air is wonderful. We had come very rapidly from the Chalet Bérard. It is generally accounted a four hours' walk to the summit; we had pursued our favourite plan of going slowly, but steadily forward, without stopping to loiter or to rest, and it had taken us but little more than two hours and a half; yet, despite my exhaustion of the night before, I had not drawn a long breath. "À présent," I exclaimed joyfully to Balmat, "je n'ai plus de peur pour les grandes courses," for my mountain vigour seemed to have been suddenly restored, and I never lost it again during the rest of my autumn's campaign. But it was far too cold to linger where we were. We could not stand still a minute, but were obliged to keep running backwards and forwards to ward off frost-bite; so after staying about ten minutes at the summit — long enough to fix all that we did see indelibly in our memories — we turned to descend, and soon regained the rocks where we had quaffed our early dose of brandy. Here we parted from our hearty, good-tempered friends of the night before; they striking off to the south-west, and retracing the steps already made by our ascending feet, we turning to the north-west, and addressing ourselves to the descent upon Sixt. We worked our way down a series of wild limestone crags, and although the new snow was very deep, and lay nearly fifteen hundred feet lower on the mountain side than it did the next time I visited the scene, there were many places in which, at the bases and in the crannies of the rock, the surface was uncovered. Even at this great height there was some vegetation, and one or two Alpine plants resolutely braved the snows and cold of this elevated region, and thrust their heads through the white mantle into the keener air outside.

By and by we descended upon the top of a Col—the Col de l'Echaud—by which the traveller may avoid the summit of the Buet, and working across the shoulder which is turned towards the Bréven, may cross from the Val Orsine to Sixt without having to climb much higher than the Col de Balme. On neither occasion when I was here had I a barometer or boiling-water apparatus with me, but speaking from memory and impression only, I should estimate the height of the Col de l'Échaud at not more than from 8500 to 9000 feet. We now bade farewell to Mont Blanc, which was hidden immediately that we began to descend the valley leading down to Sixt, of which the Col de l'Échaud is the head. The rocky and precipitous structure of the Buet gives way at once to slopes of rough turf, now covered with a light mantle of snow. Here and there great beds of dark blue gentians showed through the covering, looking bluer and brighter than ever from the contrast, each with a frozen raindrop in its centre; and starting a host of marmots, some from close beneath our feet, we came at length upon a green knoll where the slope was less rapid, and where the herbage soon gave way to a luxuriant growth of alder, bilberry, and many a smaller kind of bush.

Here we had leisure to look round, and were struck with astonishment at the scene we beheld. We were in a great amphitheatre of limestone crags. On every side was nothing but calcareous rock, exhibiting all the wildest combinations which the characteristic forms of limestone crag can produce. Towards one common point the radii of formation seemed to converge, and mass after mass of rock on every side shot forth from the circumference towards the centre, rising up like an advancing wave, separated from the neighbouring wave by a tremendous and dark ravine, and ending in a sheer precipice of many a hundred feet. It was the Ghemmi formation as seen from below Leukerbad — wave after wave of limestone rock, but in slices of waves only. Between each slice and its neighbour was a black chasm, in the very depths of which, often enough, a silver stream of water fell in white shreds, and was collected in some hollow, whence it took a second leap, and afterwards perhaps a third and a fourth, until it reached the torrent below, where scores of these delicate threads are twisted together into one. Lower down, the different terraces of these wavy radii of crag are connected by steep slopes of bosky turf, trodden by no foot save that of the chamois or the marmot. Some of the ravines are, of course, not perpendicular, but all are very steep, and all dark as ink; the formation being a slaty schist, very friable, and often degenerating almost into a black mud. Wherever a ledge occurs there is the richest Alpine pasturage, and the top of every crested crag is an oasis of the most luxuriant verdure.

We stood on one of the most prolonged of the radii, and one of a system nearly equidistant from each extremity of the amphitheatre, and differing from the rest in one particular; for the green patches which surmount each terrace of rock, instead of rising up in the form of a wave, like those on either hand, slope sharply and steeply downwards, presenting at the top a narrow edge clothed with shrubs, and a rank growth of tangled grass and of the largest Alpine plants. We had to pass two or three times from one of these edges to another, across the steep and slippery ravines which separated them, before we could reach the hollow that collected the mass of the water-courses from above, and would alone conduct us safe into the valley below. The grass, and herbs, and shrubs were laden with rain and heavy dew. They were at times far above our knees, and never less than a foot in height, and we got exceedingly wet. I had lost all the nails from one side of my boots — that on which the principal stress lay in clambering down these ravines, and I had several slips, one or two of which were awkward enough, and was soon quite wet through. When once one began to slip, it was most difficult to stop. However, we met with no serious accident, and by half-past eight we were all sitting down to breakfast by the side of the clearest and sweetest of mountain torrents, and nearly at the base of all these curious formations.

We had been told that this neighbourhood was still a favourite haunt of the chamois, and that we were not unlikely to see some of them, as they descend while the dew is still upon the ground to feed upon the grass and shrubs which are so abundant here. As we came over the brow of one of the grassy ridges I have described, we saw three chamois browsing at a great distance: presently a fourth appeared, and began to descend just towards the spot where we were. It was a pretty sight to see him skipping and trotting so gracefully and lightly down places which looked like absolute precipices, and stopping every few moments to sniff the breeze and look suspiciously round him to see that all was right. I could not forbear saying to Balmat that I thought I could hardly make up my mind to pull a trigger against so beautiful a beast. Balmat, who has killed many a chamois in his day, smiled an old hunter's smile, and quietly remarked, that unless the chamois were safer from my aim than in my compunctions, he should be sorry to change places with him if I had a rifle in my hand. Fortunately we were in the shade, and we stood perfectly still; Balmat enjoining us not to stir hand or foot, nor to speak above a whisper, though the chamois was still nearly half a mile away. The pretty creature trotted gently on till within less than 200 yards of us, when all at once he caught sight of us, and instantly beat a retreat, scrambling up the rocks and leaping up the precipices with incredible agility, till he was far beyond the reach of mischief. His companions also took the alarm, and we saw no more of them.

At our halting place we enjoyed the luxury of a thorough wash, and dried our garments on the warm slabs of rock; and after a pleasant half-hour's chat, we resumed our journey gaily. A very few minutes' walk brought us to a narrow belt of magnificent fir trees, and immediately afterwards we emerged on to the Plateau des Fonds, with which I was destined soon to become so much better acquainted. The scene that there met our eyes I have already attempted to describe; but I cannot forbear extracting a few lines from a letter written very shortly afterwards to my wife, as they show the impression created by my first passage through the Vallée des Fonds, at a time when I had had no previous idea that it possessed any remarkable beauty. It is an impression which was fully shared by my friend W., who was with me, which I have seen no reason since to change, and which my wife's letters, written to friends at home, when she came to make acquaintance with it in the following year, prove to have been produced on her mind no less than on my own. "I have only time now," I wrote, "to say that I have a great deal to say of Sixt and its environs, and that never in the whole course of my wanderings have I seen anything so exquisitely and perfectly beautiful. There is not the Mont Blanc of course; but, excepting for that, Chamouni is not fit to be named in the same day with it, and I am glad to say it is a place admirably adapted for staying at, and affords occupation for weeks. I hope our next Swiss tour may begin with a long month there, and that it may be taken at no great distance of time. Why do not people go to Sixt? I have never seen a place with so many and so great attractions."

My friend W. and I were so much pleased with the valley that we sent a messenger over to R., whom we had left behind at Chamouni, to say that we should like to stay at Sixt longer than we had intended, and to beg him to come over if possible and join us. He did so, two days later, and was no less delighted with the scenery than we were.

The following year I crossed from Sixt to Chamouni by way of the Buet. The aspect of the same scenery is so different in ascending and descending, that I think it may not be out of place briefly to describe the journey, as it may enable the reader the better to judge which way he would prefer to make the excursion. The brief account I subjoin is little more than a copy of a letter written about ten days afterwards, so that its accuracy may be depended upon.

We started from Sixt, where we had been detained several days by such rain as falls only among the Alps, on the morning of the 23rd of August, 1859, about an hour after midnight. The party consisted of my friend H., my companion of 1852, Balmat, and myself. Though the moon was up she was in her fourth quarter, and her light was so smothered in dark clouds that she did but little for us, and soon after three we passed the Plateau des Fonds in the dimness of the faintest twilight. There is always something exciting and mysterious in these midnight expeditions, and the pathway to Les Fonds seemed to gain in solemnity what it lost in distinctness and detail. The grand precipices of the Buet looked loftier and more imposing than ever, as we turned aside from the path to exercise once more the pleasant sense of ownership. I pointed out to H., who had not been there before, as well as the darkness of that early hour would permit, the spot on which the chalet was to rise; and we indulged in pleasant day-dreams of anticipation, the pleasantest of which, alas! will never find an answering reality.

We then addressed ourselves to the steep ascent

that winds up the curious accumulation of wild ravines into which the lower part of the Buet is broken. It was a glorious sight to watch the grey dawn stealing over the face of nature, grizzling first the tops of the limestone crags, then slowly creeping downwards till the great amphitheatre showed itself no longer as a round unbroken formation, but a quaint assemblage of narrow precipitous cliffs, separated from one another by deep and black ravines, each streaked by its own little silvery torrent, and each surmounted by a wedge-like slope of verdure, the favourite browsing place of the chamois. Then, at length, the cold white which precedes the sunrise settled upon everything, and the whole panorama became distinct enough. It was between four and five o'clock when we saw the first pale beams of sunlight on the cliffs still far above us. The ascent lay now through rank vegetation, where the camomile, the parnassia, and other flowers which love dank spots, were growing freely and flowering with unusual vigour: next, when we had overtopped the heads of all the limestone ravines, over a wide expanse of rich Alpine pasture, where the marmot was already at his morning meal, and where the brightest gentians bloomed, each at this early hour gemmed with a single globule of pearly dew. The moment the ridge was gained, the range of Mont Blanc burst upon the view — the valley of Chamouni, shut out by the rugged masses of the Aiguilles Rouges and the Bréven, in front of which lay the deep valley of the Dioza, from whose green pastures there came up the pleasant tinkle of some two hundred cattle bells, softened by the great distance into a gentle and musical sound. When we got there between seven and eight o'clock, there was not one cloud to chequer the summer sky, so that we saw the noble view of Mont Blanc to great advantage.

I, however, was suffering from an attack of sickness and indigestion of the most violent and distressing kind. I was quite cold, in great pain, my head throbbed as if a mountain rested upon it, my knees sank beneath me, and I was very nearly as white, they said, as the snow. I felt so ill that I did not like to separate from my companions, else I should have pushed across the lower part of the Buet, crossed another shoulder (the opposite boundary of the Val Dioza), and descended at once upon the Pierre Bérard and the Tête Noire; but I was afraid to leave the others, for I thought I might sink exhausted on the way, or be attacked by giddiness in some bad place, and so be put to great straits. Besides, I fully expected that after the heavy rain of the previous days there would be mists as soon as the sun became powerful, and I was in no condition to run the risk of losing my way by myself in a fog. As to going back, that was out of the question, for my wife was by this time already on her way to Chamouni by the road, and I knew she would be alarmed if I did not make my appearance at Chamouni that night. I was anxious, indeed, to get there the first, that all things might be comfortable for her and her companions after their long day's ride. I was equally resolved that H., whose opportunities of reaching the Alps are not so frequent as my own, should get to the summit; so I concealed as well as I could the extent of my misery, and after a short rest turned to the left and set resolutely to work to climb the crags of the Buet. The snow had been falling for three days past, and was lower and deeper than usual, and we had yet three good hours' work before we could hope to reach the top, so I think I may fairly say I gave some proof of resolution. I know no mountain which gives a greater impression of vastness than the Buet. From the Col de l'Échaud to the summit, it is almost entirely bare of any vegetation except lichens and mosses, and such few plants as cling to the little ledges in the rocks. Though these are very numerous for so dreary a spot, they make no show, and to the eye the prospect seems that of an endless waste of black shaly rock, covered with its own débris. You are almost always toiling up a wide slope of this material, hollowed out a little, and enclosed between two dark ridges—not of any great height above the general mass on which you are walking, but just high enough to separate one slope from another and shut out from the view the next similar formation. The several portions of an umbrella between the different pairs of whalebone or iron rods give no bad illustration of my meaning. You never see very far above you, and whenever you reach the top of one of these couloirs, you are sure to find another above you, quite as steep as the last, and with the snow lying rather more deeply upon it.

I forget how many of these cheering prospects rose one after another to the view; whenever I asked where the summit might be, Balmat always shook his head and gave answer, "Two hours," "An hour and a half," "Encore une forte heure," or some such encouraging assurance. The view of Mont Blanc, however, and of the connected ranges, was very magnificent, and had I been in tolerable condition would have well repaid me for all the toil. But I never yet suffered as I did this day. I was faint but could not eat, thirsty but could not drink, for I was on the verge of sickness all the while. I was in pain, and tormented with headache which never intermitted for a moment; and from one o'clock in the morning till eight in the evening, all I ate or drank was three mouthfuls of meat,— the sour bread I could not touch,—a tea-spoonful of brandy, a wine-glassful of champagne, and a tumbler of lemonade. However, my companions were very careful of me, and as they could not prevail on me to let them give up the great object of the day's expedition, they waited patiently whenever I was exhausted, while I lay on my back in the snow, sometimes for a quarter of an hour at a time. In this fashion we plodded on till we came to the foot of a very steep curtain of snow hanging from the ridge which ends in the actual summit. This is generally turned by a long détour, but to me a détour of any kind seemed quite intolerable, and I proposed, as the snow was good, to assail the curtain itself. This proved to be quite practicable, and we soon found ourselves on the great cake of glacier which surmounts the precipices of the Buet. It is of great extent, and stretches on the north-west as far as the precipices overhanging the Plateau des Fonds; and, towards the north-east, to those which guard the upper valley of the Bas Giffre, and at length hem in the Fer à Cheval.

About a quarter of an hour's walk now brought us to the summit, which looked just like the last outwork of creation; for the mists had risen, as I had expected they would, and lay all about us, and one step further would have taken us neatly over a precipice of ice, ending, to all appearance, in nothing more substantial than cloud. The wind was blowing strongly from the side of the Val Dioza, and planed off the tops of the clouds as level as if they had been cut by machinery; so that it was not till we were within a few feet of the top that we could tell how completely the distant view would be obliterated. For all that, however, it was a very striking scene. Mont Blanc rose in wonderful majesty above the long banks of white cloud, and beneath them the Val Dioza, the Bréven, and the Aiguilles Rouges were seen as distinct and bright as ever; and even at this great height the tinkling of the cattle bells was wafted gently up to us on the breeze. Though it was now past eleven, and the sun high and hot, the shrewdness of the wind made it bitterly cold; but, wind or no wind, cold or no cold, I could get no further, and was obliged to lie on my back in the snow for at least a quarter of an hour before I could manage to stir another step. It was not far from mid-day when we began to descend; and, leaving our former track to the right, made towards the south or south-west. The glorious view of Mont Blanc was now just in front of us; the Aiguilles Rouges form at all times a noble range, abounding in sharp pinnacles and streaked by many lines of glacier, but now, from the quantity of fresh snow, they looked much higher and grander than they really are, and their glaciers appeared double the true size; even the Aiguille Verte, which towered above them, wore from the same cause an aspect of unusual grandeur.

Not far from the summit we found some warm and sheltered rocks, where I lay down again and dozed peacefully for half an hour, with the faint cadence of the cow-bells striking gently on the ear, and seeming to say that we were still within reach of human sympathy and help. Before I went to sleep, I looked through the telescope at the Col d'Anterne. We had been a large and most happy party at Sixt; and while we took the long round by the Buet, and my wife and another lady the least fatiguing journey by the valleys, a third detachment was to cross the Col d'Anterne, and reach Chamouni by way either of Servoz or the Bréven; and, with the quantity of fresh fallen snow, we felt a little anxious to know how they fared. No track, however, sullied the stainless white; but, when I woke and asked Balmat to look again, he said there was "une trace forte," so that we knew their cavalcade must have passed over the Col during our halt. We learned in the evening that they had had, as we feared, rather a fatiguing passage, the snow having lain nearly a foot deep on the higher parts of the pass.

We were now on the southern face of the Buet, and the weather had evidently been severer here than on the side of Sixt, for the snow became very deep. It was thoroughly softened by the noonday sun, and we constantly sank in it nearly knee-deep, so that we had a most laborious descent; but at length we came to bare and broken faces of rock, many of which were much rounded and polished by the action of extinct glaciers. We had to descend in the beds of water-courses choked by rough, angular débris, and now half filled with melting snow. Once we had to re-ascend for about fifty feet, and for the first time for many years I was obliged to ask Balmat to give me his hand. Without it I do not think I could possibly have got up. At length, however, even the half-melted, soppy snow came to an end, and the smooth faces of the *rochers moutonnés* began to be interspersed with welcome verdure. The rough turf seemed like a luxurious carpet to the feet, and presently a few bilberries appeared, and offered a welcome refreshment to the parched mouth and tongue. A long way below, but apparently just beneath our feet (so steep is the mountain), we saw a huge block of stone, part of the débris of the Buet. Close to this was a little dot of a man, and then we recognised the colour of woodwork against the stone, and knew that the Chalet Bérard was within sight and reach. I sent Balmat on ahead to order me a cup of tea, and H. and I wound slowly down the steep descent; but, on reaching the chalet about half-past two, we found I had reckoned without my host; tea was not among the delicacies thought necessary at the Chalet Bérard, and I was fain to put up with a little lemonade, the first thing that I had tasted since eight o'clock.

We did not loiter here, but soon went pounding on, my headache growing more violent at every step. The passage across the little plain was monotonous enough, but I think the descent must be far more beautiful than the ascent, for you have a richer

FROM THE RIDGE ABOVE THE CASCADE TERRACE

…santer …
… I positi…ly …
…y freely as … as … q…
…ry p…ntly diversifie… t…
…he C…cade Be…rd is app…a…
…g up to some in… …
… stom opens on the l…
… rare beauty. The t…rr…
…he torrent is half ch…
…ne, tapestried w… h b…
…by … trees springing from …
…q… t to me more exq…
…climax of its wildne… …
…, and the rich Va… …
…sked. Fagged as I was. Le… … … … …g…
…me distance out of my way to … a … view …
…he grand waterfall.

We did not stay long at the cascade, but … …
on towards the Tête Noire, which we … … …
a mile below its highest part, and it was w… … …
difficulty that I dragged my limbs up … last … de
of ascent. However, every t…k h… it… … and
the top was reached at last; and from t… … … had
nothing to do but to stroll down-hill to A…
We sent Balmat forward to try and get us … … …
carriage to Chamouni; and, when we ar… …, we

and pleasanter prospect before you; and, despite my illness, I positively enjoyed it. The larch grows pretty freely as soon as you quit the plain, and very pleasantly diversifies the colouring. By and by the Cascade Bérard is approached, a great valley leading up to some inferior member of the Buet system opens on the left, and the scene becomes of rare beauty. The narrow gorge, where the bed of the torrent is half choked with enormous blocks of stone, tapestried with beautiful moss, and crowned by fir trees springing from the cracks and interstices, appeared to me more exquisite than ever. It reaches the climax of its wildness as you come close to the cascade, and the rich Val Orsine is suddenly unmasked. Fagged as I was, I could not forbear going some distance out of my way to get a good view of the grand waterfall.

We did not stay long at the cascade, but pressed on towards the Tête Noire, which we struck about a mile below its highest part, and it was with no small difficulty that I dragged my limbs up that last mile of ascent. However, every task has its end, and the top was reached at last; and from there we had nothing to do but to stroll down-hill to Argentières. We sent Balmat forward to try and get us a return carriage to Chamouni; and, when we arrived, we found one waiting, which he had engaged for the odd sum of three francs *and ten centimes!*— a piece of bargaining which raised our already exalted opinion of Balmat's capacities. If it had been three francs and a half, or three and a quarter, we should not have thought quite so much of the exploit; but the odd tenth implied a fineness of perception on the parts both of retainer and retained, which could not fail to extort admiration. We reached Argentières soon after five, and were at Chamouni by half-past six; and, after selecting rooms and making such a toilette as I could in the absence of our knapsacks, I strolled down the road for about a mile and a half, when I had the pleasure of meeting my wife and her companion all safe and sound, and not over tired with the day's work. Half an hour afterwards the Bréven party arrived, highly delighted with the beauties of the route by which they had come; and soon after eight o'clock we were all enjoying a sociable cup of tea, and comparing the different incidents of our several journeys.

Amongst our party was a certain Dr. Crookenden, an English physician, who had taken up his residence years ago at Cannes, and to whom my wife and I had been greatly indebted in 1854. She had been taken seriously ill at St. Nicholas, and I had exhausted my simple skill without being able to afford her the slightest relief. I sent up to Zermatt in the forlorn hope that some English medical man might be among the visitors there, and late in the evening my message was announced to Dr. Crookenden on his return from a long day on the glaciers of Monte Rosa. With the greatest kindness and promptitude he came down at once, through the darkness, to St. Nicholas, and his excellent treatment soon subdued an illness which might have led to very grave results, and enabled us, after a day or two's rest, to proceed upon our journey. We had not met again till this year, 1858, when he chanced to hear in the Oberland that we were on our way to Sixt, and having nothing particular to determine the direction of his own journey, he very kindly turned his steps in our direction, and came to Sixt to renew an acquaintance of which both parties had retained a very agreeable impression. He took me in hand this evening, after my harassing day on the Buet, and applied a simple treatment, which I have often since seen tried, and always with success, (though I have never needed it myself) in cases of great internal irritation. He wrung flannels out in very hot water, till they were dry to the touch, and then applied them over the part affected, covering them with a thick wrapping of plaids or whatever was at hand, in order to keep in the heat as long as possible. In about an hour, a hard, irregular, feverish pulse, at ninety or ninety-five, was brought down to a tranquil, gentle flow of sixty-five or seventy, and a delightful drowsiness induced, and I awoke next morning without a trace of the serious indisposition of the previous day.

The passage from Sixt to Chamouni, by the Buet, is, on the whole, I think, more interesting than that from Chamouni to Sixt. Either way, the expedition constitutes a long day's work. It occupied us upwards of seventeen hours. Owing to my illness, we must have lost from an hour and a half to two hours, but not more, and even my companion, a very strong man, felt that he had had a heavy day's work. It is an expedition quite free from difficulty or danger, in fine weather, and to a practised mountaineer. I should not hesitate for a moment to take it by myself, but it requires a little knowledge of the district. The Buet is a very wild and desolate mountain, abounding in steep slopes and curtains of ice, and precipitous faces of rock, and it is singularly monotonous in its appearance. One shoulder of it is very like another, and though, of course, so long as Mont Blanc, and the Aiguille Verte, and the Col de Balme are visible, he must be a poor mountaineer indeed who would go very far wrong; yet in a mist, where those distant landmarks failed, I know no mountain of the same height on which it would be easier to lose one's way and get into difficulties.

CHAP. VI.

"Doceas iter."—VIRGIL.

THE APPROACHES TO SIXT.

CARRIAGE ROADS FROM BONNEVILLE, GENEVA AND CLUSES. — THE COL D'ANTERNE FROM SERVOZ TO SIXT. — PASSAGE ACROSS THE BRÉVEN TO CHAMOUNI. — FROM THE PLATEAU D'ANTERNE TO LES FONDS, BY THE CHEMIN DES GRASSES CHÈVRES. — THE COL DE L'ÉCHAUD. — FROM THE VALLEY OF THE RHONE TO SAMOËNS, BY THE COLS DE COUX AND DE GOLÈZE. — BEAUTY OF CHAMPÉRY. — THE COL DE SAGÉROUX. — PASSAGES TO ST. MAURICE AND MARTIGNY.

THE town of Samoëns lies very nearly half-way, as the crow flies, between Bonneville on the west and Martigny on the east. If a circle be swept round Samoëns as a centre, with a radius of about fifteen English miles, it will pass about a mile, or a mile and half, to the west of Martigny, will run through St. Maurice, Monthey, and Bonneville, and reaching some little distance beyond Chamouni, will find the Grands Mulets upon, or very near to, its circumference. In every direction except that of Bonneville, however, these twelve or fifteen miles of lineal distance represent a good day's work, and involve a great deal of climbing and descending. From Bonneville the distance by the road is about twenty or two-and-twenty miles, and as it includes the long ascent and descent between Chatillon and the valleys of the Arve and the Giffre respectively, the drive generally occupies four or five hours at the least. From Geneva there are two carriage roads, the one by way of Bonneville, the other by way of St. Jeoire, and by the eastern side of the Môle. From Chamouni the only carriage route is by way of St. Martin, Cluses, and Chatillon, a drive of between forty and fifty miles. All the other approaches to the Valley of Sixt are by mountain paths, some easily practicable for mules, others of a kind to tax the powers of even a vigorous pedestrian.

Leaving the carriage routes as sufficiently indicated by the foregoing brief sketch, I will come to the mountain passes which lead to Samoëns or Sixt. Of these, the best known perhaps is the Col d'Anterne. There is a great wild ridge, called La Chaine des Fys, of which the easternmost extremity is the Pointe de Salles, so grand an object from the Vallée des Fonds, and the westernmost the Aiguille de Varens, above St. Martin. The actual Col d'Anterne is a point not exactly in this chain, but in a subsidiary ridge connecting the Chaine des Fys and the Buet; it is situated just to the east of their point of junction, and is commanded by a series of precipices, belonging to the Chaine des Fys, hardly second in magnificence to the Pointe de Salles. The Col d'Anterne is one of the blackest, barrenest, and most desolate spots in the world, though even here the mountain *arnica*, the *Ranunculus glacialis*, and a few other hardy plants, show what ungrateful soil nature will do her best to brighten and beautify. For a considerable distance on either side of the summit of the pass, wildness and rugged grandeur are the characteristics of the scene. Nestled beneath the precipices of Les Fys, a few hundred feet below the Col, on the Sixt side, is the Lac d'Anterne, a small lake, perhaps three-quarters of a mile across, of the darkest and deepest green, suggesting the ideas of fathomless depth and of intense cold. But the approaches to the valleys below are, on either side, most rich and lovely. The Lac d'Antèrne gives birth to a stream which flings itself madly down the vast rampart forming the lower boundary of the lake, and soon reaches an extensive plain, shut in between the Chaine d'Anterne on the right and the Pointe de Salles on the left as the traveller descends from the Col. This wild recess is one of the best pasturages of the district; and though the Chalets d'Anterne are so dirty that when we had bought our milk there we were very glad to carry it to a most respectful distance before drinking it, yet nowhere in the Alps is purer or sweeter milk to be met with. The profusion of wild flowers which gem the plain is no less marvellous than the vigour of their growth and the size they attain. Nor is the exit from the plateau the least attraction of the pass, for the pathway is carried through a perfect maze of huge boulders and débris, the hiding-place of the stream before it begins the series of bold leaps by which it gains the Giffre below, and then along the sloping bank of turf-clad earth which forms the buttress and support of the highest crags of the Pointe de Salles, and which is itself borne upon the vast system of precipices I have described as presenting, with their contorted strata, so remarkable an aspect towards the Vallée des Fonds. Having thus begun to cross the loftiest tier of the Pointe de Salles, the path continues in the same spirit to hug the opposite side of the range, and is carried back far into the valley that opens upon Salvagny and Sixt. It passes within earshot of the gentle murmurs of the Pleureuse, and descends towards Sixt, through a valley which the traveller, whatever his experience, will probably pronounce one of more than usual richness and luxuriance. The descent in the opposite direction leads to Servoz in a much more direct line; but on this side, also, the lower portion of the pass is of rare beauty. The expedition from Sixt to Servoz is an affair of about nine hours.

I have already mentioned how this route may be diversified, by descending from the Col d'Anterne to the Dioza, and then crossing the Bréven range, and descending by Planpraz upon Chamouni. I shall also have occasion to mention, in a subsequent chapter, how the Plateau d'Anterne may be quitted at either flank, and how the traveller may, if so inclined, reach the Eagle's Nest by the Chemin des Grasses Chèvres, and thence descend the Vallée des Fonds to Sixt. The combination of this way of climbing to the Plateau d'Anterne, and of the passage of the Bréven, affords the finest route that I know to or from Sixt. The Col de l'Échaud, leading from Les Fonds across the shoulder of the Buet to the Cascade Bérard, and so by the Val Orsine and Argentières to Chamouni, and the longer and much more laborious passage over the actual summit of the Buet, have been already described.

One more approach to Sixt from the west remains to be mentioned, and that is from Maglan, a few miles above Cluses on the Chamouni road, by way of the Lac de Gers. This cannot occupy above six or seven hours, and is practicable for mules on the Sixt side. Whether it be so on the side of Maglan I do not know, and should consider much more doubtful.

The most common way of passing from the valley of the Rhone to that of the Giffre, is from Monthey, just below St. Maurice, on the left bank of the Rhone, to Samoëns, by the Col de Coux and the Col de Golèze. A beautiful lateral valley, called the Val d'Illiez, opens at Monthey out of the valley of the Rhone, and runs beneath the northern base of the Dent du Midi, nearly in a straight line towards Samoëns, for a distance of about eight miles as the crow flies. Opposite to Samoëns a valley of less extent runs back from the Giffre towards Monthey. The upper end of the valley of the Dranse (a stream very different from its namesake of the Val de Bagnes, falling into the Lake of Geneva close to Thonon) insinuates itself between these two, so that in passing from the Col de Coux to the Col de Golèze, you just skirt the head of the valley of the Dranse. Neither Col is very lofty. The height of the Col de Coux, ascertained from my boiling-water observations, by taking the mean of the results given by comparison with the simultaneous barometrical readings at Geneva and at the Great St. Bernard, is 6374 English feet; that of the Col de Golèze is 5543: the difference between the results of comparison with Geneva and with the St. Bernard being in the second case thirty-four feet, and in the first only two.

I should observe that the height given by Leuthold on his map is 6067 French, or 6466 English feet, but I do not know what his authority may be; and most of the common maps are so lamentably incorrect with reference to this district, not merely in details but in matters of essential importance, that unless one knows the sources of the information they contain, the presumption is almost against their being right. I have before me a little French handbook, published at Geneva in 1856, and entitled "Souvenirs de Sixt," in the map attached to which the height of the Col de Coux is given as 6500 French, or 6927 English feet, and that of the Col de Golèze as 6280 French, or 6693 English feet. This would give a difference of elevation of only 234 feet instead of 831, as I make it. The most inexperienced eye would see at a glance, from the Col de Golèze, that my estimate of the difference between the two heights is far nearer to the truth. In Rudolf Gross's map, the height of the Col de Coux is given at 6250 French feet; but, as the Col is confounded with another leading in a totally different direction, it is obvious that his authority on the subject is worth nothing. In my calculations I have taken the height of the barometer at Geneva, with which comparison is made, to be 408 metres, or 1256 English feet; and the height of that at the St. Bernard to be 2478·34 metres, or 8131 English feet; these figures having been obligingly furnished to me by M. Plantamour, of the Observatory of Geneva.

We started from Bex to cross by the Val d'Illiez to Samoëns, on the afternoon of the 25th September, 1858. We had been so wet on the passage of the Diablerets the day before, that it was not till four o'clock that our things were dry enough to enable us to get off. Though the valley opens just opposite to Bex, we had to drive up to St. Maurice to find a bridge across the Rhone, and then back again along the opposite side of the river to Monthey, where the good road comes to an end, and we had to exchange our comfortable carriage and pair for a rough mountain char. This is a wonderful country for rules and regulations, and at Monthey they have a rule that no mule- or carriage-driver shall be bound to start within an hour of the time at which he is hired. The people at the inn tried very hard to persuade us to give up the idea of going further, and seemed very reluctant to furnish us with the means of doing so; but our plans were settled, and we resolved to adhere to our original intention. We walked outside the village and sat down by the roadside, while my wife sketched the magnificent view of the valley and the mountains opposite. Whether owing to a mistake, or perhaps to punish us for our contumacy, they kept us waiting very nearly two hours; and the sun went down, tinging the Dent de Morcle and yesterday's fresh snow on the peaks of the Diablerets with glorious crimson hues. It was nearly seven when our clumsy conveyance overtook us, and we set forth on what they called a "four hours'" journey to Champéry. The daylight was soon gone, and we saw but little of the grey granite "blocks of Monthey," so abundant here in the woods, and so interesting to the geologist, as helping him to mark out the limit of the icy stream which once flowed hither and deposited them, sharp as when they were severed from their parent peaks high upon the mountain-side. The daylight was soon gone; but, fortunately, the full September moon rose presently in all her harvest splendour from behind the Dent du Midi, and lighted up the valley we were ascending with a soft flood of silver radiance.

At first the scenery seemed simply pretty, and we thought we did not lose much by the want of a more perfect light. After a time, however, we came to wilder bits, and were sorry we could not see them by the light of day. It was a cold ride, and oftentimes the pathway was so steep that it was all the mule could do to drag up the car with my wife and our scanty baggage in it. In due time, however, Champéry was reached, just as the clock of the village church was sounding the half-hour between nine and ten, and we were welcomed most hospitably at the excellent hotel, then just newly built, where we met with a cordial reception, that seemed the pleasanter by contrast with the very cold and reluctant service accorded to us at Bex the night before, when we arrived, about the same hour, in pitiable plight, after having been exposed since mid-day to such rain and wind as falls and blows only among the mountains.

The next morning we woke to find the sun already up, and seeming to chide us for being still abed; and on turning out were gladdened by a scene of exquisite beauty. Before us fell away verdant swelling slopes of fine turf dotted with trees and chalets, and bounded by a remarkable wall of rock, which sweeps round in somewhat of a semicircular form, as if to protect the luxuriant pastures beneath it. It is almost perpendicular, about 150 feet high, and marked with lines of stratification almost as regular as courses of masonry. Above this are more green pastures, and then the steeper slopes of the Dent du Midi, partly clothed with dark pine woods, and surmounted by the tremendous precipices which are seen so distinctly from Vevey and Lausanne. To the right, between the Dent du Midi and another fine mass of rock similar in character, is a deep and narrow valley, disclosing tier after tier of naked rock, rising one behind another, each streaked with an ever-dwindling silver thread of water, in an almost interminable vista, leading up at length to the noble snowy peaks called Les Tours de Sallières, beneath which lies the pass of the Sagéroux. The path by which we mounted to the Col de Coux was so beautiful that we almost involuntarily began somewhat to disparage, in comparison with it, the scenery of Les Fonds. The next day's experience showed us that our own valley had nothing to fear from the comparison, but we ever afterwards deliberately placed Champéry second, and

second only, to Les Fonds, on the list of beautiful spots that we have visited together. It is astonishing how completely the loveliest spots often appear to escape the general attention. In Murray's "Handbook" (1854), there is not even a passing allusion to the beauty of the Val d'Illiez. Yet I can hardly conceive a pleasanter place to stay at than Champéry; there is an excellent *pension* and hotel, and the charges are quite moderate. The only objection I could find to it for a place to stay the autumn in, is that it must be hot.

The ascent of the Col de Coux is perfectly easy, and though we did not start from Champéry till after eight, we were on the top before eleven o'clock. The bottom of the valley between the Col de Coux and the Col de Golèze is occupied by a large fir wood, containing some of the finest trees we have met with on our travels. I measured one of the boles about five feet from the ground, and found it to be eighteen feet in circumference. At the foot of one of the great firs we came upon an enormous ants' nest, a cone four feet high. After passing through this wood we defiled for a short distance beneath a lofty precipice of limestone crags, marked by curiously-twisted lines of stratification, both ends of a tolerably regular and horizontal ellipse being presented by different parts of the formation. Two hours after leaving the Col de Coux we reached the summit of the second Col, about 800 feet lower, according to my measurements, than the Col at the head of the Val d'Illiez.

Some chalets are grouped close to the Col de Golèze, and we were able to buy some excellent milk, some indifferent wine, and some coarse bread and cheese, upon which we made a very tolerable lunch. We then descended to Samoëns, now in the path, now out of it, through wild woodland scenery, which has dwelt in our recollection as amongst the most exquisite with which our wanderings have made us acquainted. Sometimes we wound our way through beech woods so deep as almost to exclude the light of day, and quite to shut out every glimpse of the bold rocky flanks of the valley we were in. Sometimes we tripped lightly down over slopes and knolls of the greenest and softest grass, broken here and there by a little patch of trees, in the midst of which nestled a chalet of russet brown, or rising into a gentle eminence on which was perched a sunburnt barn or cowshed. We could scarcely resist the temptation which presented itself at every moment, to stray into the green embowered alleys that opened every here and there on either side of our descending way. Whenever we emerged from the trees the prospect we had before us was the smiling valley of Samoëns, basking in sunshine, beneath a layer of fleecy clouds that lay upon the mountain tops; once or twice we saw the lofty summit of the Pointe de Salles peep out for a moment above that sea of mist. About two hours and a half were thus pleasantly spent between the Col de Golèze and Samoëns: we reached the latter place at half-past four, and driving on at once to Sixt, brought our easy day's journey to an end before sunset.

The Col de Sagéroux, which I have mentioned before as one of the passages from the valley of the Rhone to Sixt, leads from Champéry beneath Les Tours de Sallières to the Fond de la Combe, and thence by the char road past the Fer à Cheval to Sixt. It was formerly a pass difficult, and even dangerous in certain states of the weather, but I believe it may now be safely traversed under all ordinary circumstances. I have always heard it spoken of as an excursion of great interest, but I am not yet personally acquainted with it.

There are also, I believe, passages leading from the most accessible parts of the amphitheatre of the Fer à Cheval directly to St. Maurice and to Martigny: judging from the districts amongst which they must conduct the traveller, they can hardly fail to be grand in themselves, and to command extensive and distant prospects, but I have never even met with any person who knew anything about them.

CHAP. VII.

> . . . "He pry'd through Nature's store
> ∗ ∗ ∗ ∗ ∗ ∗ ∗ ∗
> What she had hidden 'neath her verdant floor,
> The vegetable and the mineral reigns."
> THOMSON.
>
> " Sweet specimens ! which toiling to obtain
> He split great rocks, like so much wood, in twain."
> MRS. HEMANS.

THE FOSSILS OF MOËD.

FROM SERVOZ TO MOËD.—LES ÉBOULEMENTS.—THE VAL DIOZA.— MOËD.—THE FOSSIL BED.—A STORM ON THE MOUNTAINS.—A NARROW ESCAPE.—AN INCIDENT OF THE STORM ON THE MER DE GLACE.—SECOND VISIT TO MOËD.—FROM CLUSES TO SIXT.—LES FONDS IN THE MORNING.—CHEMIN DES GRASSES CHÈVRES.—FOSSIL TEETH.—RENDEZVOUS AT MOËD.—INTERIOR OF A CHALET.— HOW WE PASSED THE NIGHT.—SUNRISE.—OUR COOK.—A SECOND NIGHT IN THE CHALET.—DESCRIPTION OF THE FOSSILS.—SPRINGING A MINE.—DESCENT TO THE DIOZA.—ASCENT OF THE BRÉVEN.— A COOL PATH.—A TOILETTE ON THE SNOW.—CHAMOUNI.

IN the autumn of 1857 I spent upwards of six weeks at Chamouni and in the neighbourhood, and soon after I arrived, Balmat made known to me that he had found, some two years before, a bed of very beautiful fossils, chiefly ferns, not very far from the summit of the Col d'Anterne, and that he had kept the information to himself ever since, in order, as he was kind enough to wish, that we might, as it were, share the honours, though we certainly could not share the merits, of the discovery. There were so many other excursions to be made, however, that it was not till Tuesday, the 8th of September, that we were able to set off on our exploring expedition. We took with us a worthy man, Jean Michel Bellin,— the same who is mentioned in my " Wanderings " as having acted as porter for us when my wife and I camped out on the Mer de Glace,— as we wished to be able to blast the rock, and he is the only miner in the valley of Chamouni. The nearest way lies over the Bréven, whence you descend into the valley of the Dioza behind, and crossing the stream mount again 1500 or 2000 feet on the opposite side. But I wished to see the commencement of the passage of the Col d'Anterne, as taken from Servoz, and I was desirous also of reaching the destined spot as early as possible in the day. We therefore walked down to Servoz and slept there. By four o'clock the next morning we were on our way towards the Col d'Anterne. The weather was very threatening, and soon after we started the rain came on to pour so hard that we were obliged to halt and to shelter for the best part of an hour under the broad eaves of a chalet.

It was significant of the early hour at which we were abroad that, although we were leaning against the cottage and chatting all the while, we did not appear to disturb anybody; and we left the village to which it belonged soon after five, without having attracted the notice of any one but a stray cur or two, who came barking at our heels as only the Alpine curs can do. We pushed on steadily, exposed sometimes to very angry showers, but still with intervals of finer weather long enough for us to get tolerably dry again. I cannot say I have retained any very vivid impression of the scenery. As we ascended, the clouds settled on the peaks and ranges above us, and everything looked gloomy and dreary enough. There is a magnificent limestone range, called the Chaine des Fys, which drops abruptly perhaps a couple of thousand feet, in a series of stupendous precipices, just above the Col d'Anterne, and we were working our way along the slopes at the base of this range, in a direction nearly parallel with it. From one part of the chain, at some former time, a vast avalanche of rocks and stones has descended, and strewn the side of the mountain with its enormous débris for a length and breadth of many miles. The only place where I have seen traces of such wholesale mountain disintegration is on the passage of the Diablerets, where the same striking phenomenon has taken place on even a larger scale. The tract which is here covered with the ruins of a mountain is called " La Montagne des Éboulements," and very rough and fatiguing we found it.

The place for which we were bound is not upon the pathway to the Col d'Anterne, but a little nearer to the head of the Val Dioza (the wild valley which lies to the north of the range of the Bréven), and about a thousand feet, so far as I can remember, below the summit of the Col. The upper part of the Val Dioza is narrow enough, but lower down it widens considerably; the range of the Bréven, and the chain which runs from the Buet and abuts upon the Chaine des Fys at the Col, forming a kind of V,— the angle being just beneath the massive structure of the Buet. The aperture, however, between the two arms of the V, as it widens out, is not occupied by a plain through which the Dioza meanders, but that stream hugs the left-hand stroke of the letter, and pursues its fretful course close beneath the Bréven, while from the right-hand stroke a spur is pushed forward, which occupies the greater part of the opening. It rises indeed to a very considerable height, just opposite to the top of the Cheminée of the Bréven,— the spot to which tourists generally ascend,— and falls away above the stream in a series of abrupt and formidable precipices, between which and the Bréven the Dioza is left with very little space indeed to spare. Our way lay across the neck or depression between the Col d'Anterne and this subsidiary offshoot, and after passing through this opening we had to descend a short distance, when we found ourselves amongst the cluster of huts called the Chalets of Moëd, wonderfully dirty, and tenanted then only by women, children, and pigs,—the pigs forming the most numerous, and apparently the most important, portion of the population. It was as well for us that the men were all out looking after the sheep or cattle on the mountain sides, for we wished to be at liberty to pursue our researches without being interfered with; and we thought it likely enough that if any of the men followed us, and saw what we were about, they would fancy we had found a gold mine, and disturb the specimens we intended to leave for a more favourable opportunity of bringing back.

The fossil bed is a little higher than the chalets,

and a little nearer to the head of the valley. It lies in a narrow ravine — scarcely more than a scar on the surface of the mountain — the channel of an insignificant little watercourse; and the productive portion is certainly not more than a hundred yards from top to bottom. It is extraordinary how Balmat should have found it out, and still more so how, having been there but once before, he should have remembered its position so accurately, that though there seems nothing to distinguish it from fifty other little ravines in the same neighbourhood, he walked straight to it without the loss of a yard. But Balmat has a most faithful and retentive memory, and goes about with his eyes open to everything that is worth looking at; and one day, as he was making his way from Chamouni to the Col d'Anterne, by way of the Bréven and the Val Dioza, he picked up, near the banks of that stream, a bit of black shaly stone, about a couple of inches square, in which he observed a few fragments of a different colour. On looking at this more closely, he was convinced they were bits of vegetable fibre of some kind, in a fossil state, and he came to the conclusion that where these came from something better would be found. He was close to a little torrent at the time, and resolved not to quit its course. Every here and there he picked up another and another bit of the same kind of substance, or intermixture of substances, and patiently hunting these indications up to their origin, he came at last, a good fifteen hundred feet above the place where he had found the first of them, upon a narrow outcropping thread of slaty schist, washed and polished by a tiny rill of water, beneath whose transparent medium fern-leaves, as perfect as when they were first imbedded, tinted, some apparently with the natural green, others with a golden lustre, greeted his eye and rewarded him for his patient search.

It was about eight o'clock when we arrived, and we soon selected a favourable spot to work at, and began chipping out specimens. There was no difficulty in finding them, for the whole rock seemed to be composed of them. They lay oftentimes twenty and thirty caked together in the thickness of an inch, and wherever you split a piece of the substance a fresh set of fossils was disclosed. We worked hard for several hours, and selected a great variety of beautiful specimens, which we laid aside to be brought over to Chamouni by porters. Towards two o'clock, however, the weather, which had been showery all day, showed unmistakeable signs of a heavy storm. Old Bellin, who was quite as much interested in the matter as ourselves, made up his mind to pass the night at the chalets, and to stay where he was, and quarry on as long as the weather would allow him: we were to return to Chamouni that night, and send over men for the cargo of fossils we had laid on one side. Balmat filled his handkerchief with some of the most exquisite of the smaller pieces, and I did the same with mine, and bidding good-bye to our indefatigable friend Bellin, we turned homewards, passing above the Chalets of Moëd, so as to escape at once the filth of its alleys and the curiosity of its inhabitants.

We were just crossing the little ridge from which we had descended upon Moëd in the morning, when the storm burst upon us in all its fury. We were wet to the skin before we had gone fifty yards, and thought we could hardly be exposed to worse weather. However, it did not last very long, and the sun came out brightly afterwards, and we were beginning to feel a little less draggled and uncomfortable, when we observed dense masses of black cloud rolling up the valley with amazing rapidity, and darting forth at intervals lurid flashes of forked lightning. I never saw a storm come up so fast. Almost before we had time to think of it, the rush, as of a whirlwind, was upon us, and with a shriek and a howl the tempest wrapped us in its murky folds. The hail and the rain pelted horizontally into our faces. We could not see a hundred yards in any direction, and the lightning played about us — apparently quite close, for there was no perceptible interval between the flash and the report. Electrical considerations would have counselled us to let our sticks go, and ourselves to lie down; but the storm was accompanied by a sudden lowering of the temperature; the blast swept through us, and to lie down would have been to die of cold and exhaustion — and we knew of at least one watercourse that *must* be crossed. It was true that we had passed it without wetting our feet in the morning; but such rain as this, we feared, would turn it into a torrent that it would be hopeless to attempt to leap without our sticks; so we did the best we could, by carrying them nearly level, with the point a little downwards, and happily escaped without injury from the lightning.

The storm was a very protracted one, and long after that portion which was so highly charged with electricity had passed by, we continued to be enveloped in a dense and driving rain, which prevented our seeing whither we were going, and but for what we had passed through, the lightning and thunder would have been fearful. However, there was no great danger of losing our way. We knew the torrent was on our right, and that we must strike it as early as we could, if we were to get across it in safety — and we knew also that we had no business to go uphill. We were not long, therefore, in reaching the stream; but how changed from the little rivulet of clear water, just murmuring as it bounded lightly from stone to stone, that we had scarcely more than strided across a few hours ago! It was now eight or nine feet wide, full four feet deep in dark liquid mud, and rolling down, in its wild rage, great blocks of stone, as if they had been playthings. The sound of the masses which were tumbled over and over, as it came up dull and muffled out of the thick and discoloured flood, was really awful. Balmat leaped across it, with the help of his stick, and just landed on the other side. He turned at once and shouted something to me at the top of his voice, which I understood to be "Dangereux! dangereux!" and, as I thought, waved his hand in warning. I bawled out in reply, that if he would stay where he was, I would seek a passage higher up, and come down and join him. I thought he made a sign of acquiescence, and went up by the side of the torrent, forcing my way with great difficulty. In about ten minutes I came to a place where the channel forked into two, and now attacking the enemy's forces in detail, I won my way across easily enough, and made all haste to the place where I had left my companion.

In order to approach it I had to descend a very steep ravine of slaty débris, covered with a rank and dripping vegetation. I had not gone far before I slipped, and shot down some fifty feet without being able to check myself at all. I clung to my fossils as long as I could; but I was in danger, for just below me was the black and angry flood, perceptibly swollen within the last quarter of an hour, and the dead weight of my bundle of stones was a serious addition to the forces that were dragging me to the brink of destruction. Had I gone but a few feet further, and slipped into the torrent, I should have been "perdu sans ressource," as Balmat had warned me when we were on the other side; and I believe he spoke nothing but the literal truth. So I was obliged to let my burden go, and in a moment it was engulphed and swept away. Fortunately, now that I had my hands more at liberty, and had parted with this incumbrance, I was able to stop myself, though my hands were much cut by the effort; but I was not more than four or five feet from the stream when I did so. If I had left my stick when we were in the thunder-cloud, I must have perished here. The water might or might not have been deep enough to take me overhead, but it would not have been a question of swimming. I should have been knocked to pieces between the water and the rocks.

I crept cautiously enough along the bank of débris, and soon reached the spot where I had left Balmat; but he was gone! I shouted as loud as I could, but my voice was drowned in the roar of the wind and the torrent, and if he had been twenty yards off, I doubt if he would have heard me. I waited nearly a quarter of an hour, at what I had considered the trysting place, but at length I was so cold that I dared not wait any longer. The rain and hail were horizontal, and the artillery of heaven was still playing fearfully about and around me. I climbed painfully and anxiously up the ravine where I had so nearly come to a bad end, and reached some turf-slopes above. Here I wandered backwards and forwards, shouting minute signals to Balmat, but in vain; and at length I thought it safer to go on. I knew my direction, and had descended some distance when a lift in the mist took place, though the rain continued: I thought it a good opportunity to look for Balmat, and went back a long way. I could see nothing of him, and very soon the mists came swooping down again, and I turned homewards in good earnest. In about half an hour I came upon Balmat, sheltering under a rock—one of the "éboulements"—and waiting for me in great anxiety. It appeared that when I thought he said "dangereux," he had only used the milder phrase, "pas trop bon,"—that he had understood me to say I would go round, but not that he was to wait where he was, and that he had shouted in reply: "You will find the path a little way above; take that, and I will wait for you there;" and he had thought I made signs to say I understood: yet we were only some ten feet apart. Of course we had not parted two minutes before we were out of sight of one another.

We now plodded homewards, and for the last half hour before we reached Servoz the weather was fine, and I remember being struck with the extreme beauty of the descent, through woods of rich and variegated foliage — now pouring, rather than dripping, after the recent storm, — with the green slopes of the Col de Voza and the Forclaz rising beyond the plain of the Arve. On this descent we overtook a lady who had been crossing the Col d'Anterne, and had been, like ourselves, exposed to the full fury of the tempest on the bare and shelterless mountain side. She looked fearfully wet and draggled, and her clothes hung about her in close heavy folds, which seemed to tie her up as she walked. She had been obliged to come down from her mule, and even when dismounted she was once carried fairly off her legs by the blast.

It is wonderful how such bad weather, to use a common phrase, "takes it out of one." I have scarcely ever felt such mortal fatigue as when I was toiling back along that somewhat monotonous bit of road between Les Ouches and Chamouni. I hardly knew how to get one leg in front of the other, or how, when I had accomplished that, to drag the other after it.

We heard the next day of an incident that occurred on the Mer de Glace that evening which might have led to consequences of a very serious nature. Two young men, with whom I had dined the day before, started in the morning, but not very early, on account of the threatening aspect of the weather, for the Col du Géant. They got as far as the great snow-basin above the Séraques, when a blinding mist drove in from over the Col. They had told me what difficulty they had had in procuring decent guides. Those who came next on the rota when they applied happened to be a very ragged set, and the chief guide declared that the regulations should not be infringed upon. By dint of patient waiting and watching, they managed to escape the worst of them, but were obliged to put up with men of whom only one, I think, had made the passage before, and none of whom inspired them with any confidence. In the obscurity, their conductors lost their way, and nightfall caught them still wandering about the great basin of the Géant. They were obliged to huddle together for warmth, and to pass the hours of darkness as best they might upon the ice. During the night it cleared, after some hours of truly fearful rain, and they were able to grope their way back through the difficult passage of the Séraques. They reached the Montanvert at half-past three in the morning, half dead with cold and exposure. I did not see them myself, but I spoke with a person who had heard the story from their own lips.

We sent over porters who fetched the fossils we had left by the side of the rivulet; and a day or two afterwards, being about to revisit Sixt, made arrangements with old Bellin and one of his sons to meet us at Moëd on Tuesday the 15th of September, with provisions for two or three days, as we had seen enough only to whet our curiosity, and were anxious to make a more thorough examination of the contents of Balmat's fossil bed. The people at the chalets had quitted them the day after the storm, and betaken themselves to less elevated habitations, but there would be plenty of hay and probably some fire-wood left, and Bellin would know to whom they belonged, so that we could make compensation for what we consumed; and with these aids we hoped to sleep pretty comfortably in one of the deserted chalets. It may be useful to some reader to know about how much food is needed for such an expedition, so I will give the list of our articles of consumption. The party was to consist of Balmat, old Bellin, and myself, and we expected one at least of Bellin's sons would be backwards and forwards, carrying fossils to Chamouni, and we therefore had to be ready for him also. We intended to spend two days and a half at the chalets. We ordered, therefore, one shoulder and three " pièces " (hunks of three or four pounds each) of mutton, a small bit of tongue, four loaves, two pounds of cheese, one pound of butter, three pounds of sugar, half a pound of coffee, a quarter of a pound of tea, some salt, a bottle of boiled cream, three bottles of old St. Jean, and a pint of brandy. Our " service " consisted of one coffee-pot and one cup.

Balmat and I left Chamouni on the Friday after our first expedition to Moëd, and slept again at Servoz. We went on the second occasion to the less fashionable hotel — the Hotel de l'Univers — where we were incomparably more comfortable, and were charged only about half what we paid at the other. Starting soon after daybreak, in a char of the country which was going down to market, we rode to St. Martin for three francs! and after breakfasting there, hired a trap to take us on to Cluses, whence we walked to Samoëns. The walk from Cluses into the valley of the Giffre is even more beautiful than that from Bonneville. The first hour's journey is a steep climb through richly cultivated slopes, where the quantity of fruit trees and of fruit upon them, when we passed, was really prodigious. At every turn you come upon clumps of ash, chestnut, beech, oak, elm, and other forest trees, all of very fine growth, and intermingled in the most agreeable fashion. In two places there were narrow lanes cut in deep thickets of beech, so shady and so tempting that one might have passed the day beneath the arching foliage, and not been weary. We slept at Samoëns, and on the Sunday moved up to Sixt, where we revisited twice the beautiful Vallée des Fonds.

o

On the appointed Tuesday morning we started from Sixt about half-past six, and we agreed, instead of taking the usual path to the Col d'Anterne, to go once more up the valley of which we could never have enough, and see how the Plateau des Fonds looked by the morning sun — it had always been towards mid-day when I had been there hitherto. When we reached the bridge below it, I proposed to Balmat that instead of taking the pathway to the left, we should make our way by the side of the torrent which pours wildly down through a black ravine on the right. The grass was wet with rain which had fallen in the preceding night, but the sun was now shining out of a sky of cloudless blue, and we wound our way up the ravine, through groups of firs and beeches, with the clear stream dashing in a broken course beside us. Presently we crossed a little lateral ravine — now the boundary of my property — and entered upon a slope once richly clad with firs, but now denuded of most of them. Here a beautiful little cascade, fringed with a rich growth of ferns and water-loving plants, lent an additional charm to the scene; but what struck me particularly was the wonderful quantity of wild fruit to be had for the gathering. Even at this late period of the season, strawberries, bilberries, raspberries, and stone-bramble-berries were flourishing in the wildest profusion, and afforded us an ample and luscious early dessert. I have before me now a tracing of a wild strawberry, which I made on the spot; it was an inch in length, and more than two inches round the widest part.

Presently we rejoined the track leading to the Buet; but, as soon as we had crossed the stream which comes from the Col de l'Échaud, we turned sharply to the right and followed an ascending pathway, running back along the side of the valley in the direction of the Pointe de Salles. Along this path, called " Le Chemin des Grasses Chèvres," are to be found the most magnificent firs and larches that this district produces; it leads up to a wild plain lying beneath the southern precipices of the Pointe de Salles, where are situated the chalets and the pasturages d'Anterne, and across which the regular passage from Sixt to Servoz by the Col d'Anterne is carried. We might have followed the Chemin des Grasses Chèvres to its junction with the path to the Col d'Anterne, and have ascended to the top of the Col and thence descended upon Moëd; but we preferred, after a very short time, to strike directly up the mountain side, and make as nearly as we could in a straight line for the point of the ridge just above the chalets. All at once, to our surprise, we emerged on to the top of one of those wild crests of limestone I have attempted to describe when speaking of the way to the Buet, and stood on a narrow ridge clad with bushes and brambles to the very brink of the precipices—many hundred feet deep—on either side. We looked long for chamois, but it was too late in the day to meet with them so low as this. We found a large ants' nest, with a cone some eighteen inches high, very near the end of the narrow ridge of rock.

We now crossed for half an hour some broken ground, partly peat, partly turf, partly of rough stones, till we reached a long, gentle, uniform slope, where all vegetation ceased, and a black wilderness of débris and broken shale presented anything but an inviting aspect. Balmat began to hunt keenly for fossils, as we were approaching a fossil district, and he told me that not far from here he had once picked up a fossil tooth three inches long, which the Genevese naturalists pronounced to be a hippopotamus's. We had not gone many steps before my eye lighted on a tooth about two inches long, so white, and in such a perfect state of preservation, that I supposed it to be some sheep's or cow's tooth recently dropped there; and, pointing to it, I said, laughing, "Here, Balmat, you want teeth; I have found you one already;" but, on picking it up, it turned out to be a genuine fossil; though, if it ever belonged to a hippopotamus, he must have been a small one. We spent a long time foraging on this and the succeeding slopes, and in the intervening ravines, and found many belemnites and ammonites—amongst them some very perfect specimens. All the best specimens, however, were so deeply imbedded in the large pieces of rock, that, without hammer or chisel, we had no chance of cutting them out.

We struck the ridge, and were greeted with the grand prospect of Mont Blanc, about a mile or two to the east of the Col d'Anterne and at a higher elevation, and had a very long walk round the great shoulders of turf-covered rock which descend towards the valley of the Dioza. The number of marmots that we started was extraordinary, and some of them were so fat that they could scarcely waddle to their holes. Their shrill whistle resounded in our ears at every moment. At length, after eight hours' walking, we reached our fossil bed, hungry and thirsty enough, for we had brought nothing with us but a scrap of tongue which a worthy farmer at Servoz, who had tried his best to make us drunk (and had succeeded wonderfully well in the attempt upon himself), had insisted upon Balmat's taking away with him, and which we ate on the mountain side without any bread, slaking our thirst with our own extemporised lemonade, a beverage not to be despised, concocted out of citric acid, sugar, lemon essence, and water.

There was no one at the rendezvous, but we were cheered by seeing Bellin's tools lying about, and presently we saw him and his son François emerge from one of the chalets at about ten minutes' walk from us. Balmat shouted in patois, as a ravenous Alpine man only can shout, that we were an hungered; whereupon Bellin turned back into the chalet, and presently afterwards an excellent lunch made its appearance. We then set to our task, and worked hard all the afternoon, trying new places higher up and lower down, and getting every now and then into a vein of fresh plants. There is no work much harder than sitting with one's back bent half double, splitting and chipping stones with a chisel and hammer. About six o'clock, having had enough of it, we knocked off work and went down to the chalets. There were about forty of one sort or another, so that there were a good many to choose from; but there was one, Bellin said, which was considered the cleanest and best, whither any chance wayfarer was always recommended to resort for a night's lodging; so of course we chose that. I will try to give some idea of our quarters.

The whole building is about twenty feet by fourteen. The walls, for a height of six or seven feet, are made of rough undressed stone. Above that the structure is of wood. The larger part of the ground floor is taken up by the cow-shed, but a space of about fourteen feet by six is left for " parlour and kitchen and all." This part is open from the floor to the roof, the cow-shed part being timbered over with undressed fir-poles, and the part above it being reserved for sleeping accommodation and for a store-place for anything there may be to keep. A rough ladder about eight feet high gives access from the house-place to this upper story. The " parlour and kitchen and all " is divided by a rickety partition from the cow-shed, which opens out of it by a narrow door; it is itself portioned off into two parts—one of which, about eight feet by six, is the living-place; the other is the pantry, larder, store-room, and wine-cellar. There is no chimney and no fireplace. The fire is made on the earth, or rather rock, for the floor is a broken mixture of earth and rough rock, in which rock predominates. The smoke finds its own way out, chiefly by the door; and past your eyes, wherever you may chance to be. There is no lack of ventilation, for the gable opposite to the parlour-end is made of planks, fixed about two or three inches apart, so as to admit air and rain very freely. The smell of the departed cows still hangs fragrantly about the place, and the filth collected outside at the cow-house end is a serious obstacle to your working your way out to the clean part of the rivulet running by its side, to find which you must get quite clear of the village. There is one small flap-table folded up against the partition between the house-place and the cow-shed: it has one leg to support it; there are two four-legged benches and one three-legged stool to sit upon, and voilà the furniture.

We have brought tea and sugar and boiled cream, but, alas, how to make tea! I have provided a coffee-pot, but Balmat pronounces it soft-soldered, and fears it will not stand fire. There is only one pot—"marmite" as the Chamouni men call it in patois—of any kind, discoverable in the village, and that has been used to make soup for the pigs, and has never been cleaned since, and is of so strong a flavour that Balmat says it has actually made his head ache—a fact confirmed by young Bellin, who comes in from an independent tour of discovery complaining of a headache from the stench of the "marmite." In despair we put the coffee-pot to the test. All honour to its immortal maker! Soft-soldered or hard, it stands the ordeal, and we boil up a decoction of tea in it, as we had done years before at the chalets of the Mattmarksee, and at our bivouac at the head of the Mer de Glace.

Meanwhile, however, a shout of triumph from without announces that that enterprising discoverer, young Bellin, nothing daunted by nightfall, has continued his investigations, and has found a prize in a distant chalet. Presently he appears, laden with the spoil, two "marmites," both tolerably clean, and a perfect mine of cups and plates, about the texture of coarse flower-pots. The one cup from Chamouni is now put religiously aside for "Monsieur," or "Monche," as I am more often called in patois, and "marmites" and "asshiettas" are thoroughly washed, and water set to boil over the fire. It now gets quite dark, after a superb sunset, in which Mont Blanc has been lit up with the glorious ruddy light that Alpine adventurers, careful of the signs of the weather, love to see, and which to-night dwells fondly on the solemn summit, long, long after every lower peak has ceased to glow. And now we find we have no light but the fire! with all our care, we have never thought of the candles. Balmat is "désolé" at the extent of the inconvenience to me, who make and think very light of it, and rather enjoy the fun, until a something reminds me that I am in a chalet. I have been overcome with fatigue, and have sat me down incautiously on the bench and leaned against the partition; and I began to think not quite so hopefully as before of what the night would be. After tea, about eight o'clock, we lit some sticks of dry wood to make a little light, and Balmat and old Bellin "arranged" my couch. It looked like hay, but turned out to be a substance peculiar to chalets—a mixture, about half and half probably, of hay and fleas. I turned in fully dressed, except my boots and hat, and presently three burrowing animals near me settled into *their* places, and before long we all four fell asleep, notwithstanding all our little discomforts, and slept with varying perseverance and success, and with differing lucid intervals, till five o'clock on Wednesday morning. Whenever I was awake I heard the mice scuttering about in all directions, and Balmat declared that one passed close to his face. The first who stirred was Balmat; and it was here as it had been at the Grands Mulets a fortnight before—the instant one moved, all the rest sprang to their feet with an alacrity which did not say too much for the comfort of our sleeping-place.

Out we turn — men, hay, fleas, and all — into a glorious crisp September morning, not a cloud in the clear sky, not a speck of mist on mountain top or in dale or valley. I get out my little dressing-case and seek the first clean rill I can find, nearly bent double by the prickling hay, which makes me feel something like a porcupine with his quills stuck in the wrong way. It has found its way up everywhere, and seems to have constituted itself the appropriate lining of shirt, trowsers, stockings, and everything else. Here I gladly divest myself of my garments, and make that chase, so necessary after such a night, where, as Balmat feelingly remarks, " Le gibier ne manque pas ; " and, stripping to the skin upon the turf, all white and crisp with hoar-frost, indulge in a luxury so little known there that I expect to see the stream stand still. Whilst I am dressing, the palest and most transparent blush of rose suffuses the eastern sky, and even tinges the peaks of the Bréven; but it is too fine a morning for it to last, and before it can fling its transient beauty over the distant snows of Mont Blanc, a bright pale streak of light falls upon his lofty head, and gradually steals lower and lower down, till one by one the Monts Maudits, the Mont Blanc de Tacul, the Dome, and the Aiguille du Midi have caught the morning beam, and the Calotte, the Corridor, and the Côte are already drowned in a flood of light.

I leave the soap, and sponge, and brush, for Balmat's use — the Bellins are above such human frailties—and when I enter the hut again the fire is bright, the tea is made, and our small board literally groans under the weight of bread and meat, and cheese, and other good things. One meal is a good deal like another; tea and wine are the respective characteristics of breakfast and dinner, but there is little else to distinguish them. This meal is quickly despatched, and by half-past six we are ready for work. Bellin the elder, and Balmat, make for the fossils; I stay behind to attempt a sketch of the Bréven and Mont Blanc. All goes well till I come to put in the snow, when I find, alack! that though well furnished with white paint, I have never thought of the brush. I don't consider my handiwork worthy of the excessive pains and the amount of inventive skill which supplied the deficiency, in a similar case, on the Torrenthorn some three years before*, so my sketch e'en goes

* See " Wanderings among the High Alps," chap. xi.

without it, and by eight o'clock I too am at work breaking stones and my back at once. François Bellin is breaking *his* back in another way. He has started with about sixty pounds of fossils, with which pleasant load he is descending to the Dioza and will soon be mounting the Bréven. He is to deposit them near the chalets of Planpraz, and from there to return with a fresh bottle of boiled cream and a "bougie," that we may not be without light this evening.

All day long, from morning till nightfall, in early morning's dew, in a blazing noonday sun, and in the sultry heat of afternoon, we work steadily on. We try new ground, and Bellin the elder, our staff and stay, springs a mine and we discover some fine specimens, but not finer than what we have already chipped out from close to the surface. The stone is very brittle and yielding, and does not split kindly. We come across rare things, but cannot chip them out. One vein is christened "casse-cœur," it is so obstinate, cross-grained, and méchant; but late in the afternoon Balmat mounts again to our second place of search, and succeeds in discovering a band of fossils more beautiful than any we have yet turned up, and as it is getting towards night we agree to mine there to-morrow;

and the men set to work to arrange a new load for young Bellin's gratification, while I, being thoroughly tired and my back aching to excess, leave them to it, and taking with me the fresh cream and the candle with which the active young Bellin has just returned, descend to the chalets laden with all our meat-bones and meat débris of to-day and yesterday. I light a fire and boil the "marmite," and have just had time to break the bones up, cut the meat into little pieces and set it on the fire to simmer, when I am attracted by the loveliest sunset I have seen during the whole of this fine season. The cook, however, in a chalet and with damp wood for fuel, has no sinecure, and I had to alternate between a standing position at the door, admiring the sunset, and a kneeling position before the fire, blowing till my face was as red as my embers, and the tears trickled down my cheeks with the acrid smoke. About half-past six or seven the rest come down, and in half an hour the broth is ready, and elicits the most satisfactory panegyrics from my hungry guests. Balmat declares he finds the inn cheap, the fare excellent, and the landlord obliging, and declares his intention of patronising it himself and recommending his friends to do the same: while the Bellins, in homelier phrase, give utterance to repeated and heartfelt exclamations of "Bon, bon!" which go to the heart of the cook.

It is half-past eight before we get to roost to-night, but we do sleep, spite of the fleas and the cold, for we are all tired, and it is half-past five on Thursday morning before any one rouses. Again I turn out, in a glorious morning " which had arisen as serene and calm as the blue eternity out of which it came;" and beneath a cloudless sky, and with the hoar-frost yet upon the ground, I indulge again in the cheap luxury of a cold bath, and revel in the wonderful spectacle of which the eye and the mind never tire, — which never loses its mystery, its solemnity, its novelty,—a sunrise upon Mont Blanc. It is a sight I do not often see without calling to mind the beautiful words of a most accomplished and fervent writer: — "The grand silence of earth and skies, just broken by the faint twitter of awakening life — the pure freshness that breathes over the yet untainted world — the exquisite purple of the eastern hills edged with a silvery rim of light, deepening into broader and more lustrous gold — the pale, cold grey of receding night, where moon and stars still beautiful are dimly vanishing—the rich, influent tide of day, so different from the melting softness of its ebbing hues, that is reflected every moment with increasing sharpness from the objects over which it rolls, and that lights up as with the joyousness of hope into boundless brilliancy the dewy womb of morning — these effects, so rapid in their succession and so glorious, so like a new creation — take us back to the beginning of time, and transport us to the Eden of our first parents, and make us feel, like them, in the presence of these sublime transitions of unchanging nature, that the Spirit of the Living God is around us." *

On my return I find François Bellin already off with his heavy load, and after a quick repast we, too, repair to our posts, and I examine somewhat more carefully the little ravine or gully in which we are at work. I wish here to disclaim all pretension to geological knowledge. At the time I was at Moëd I did not know even that the first thing to be noted was the dip of a stratum like this;

---

* " Christian Aspects of Faith and Duty," by the Rev. J. J. Tayler, p. 193. (2nd edition.)

> "Should God again,
> As once in Gibeon, interrupt the race
> Of the undeviating and punctual sun,
> How would the world admire! but speaks it less
> An agency divine, to make him know
> His moment when to sink and when to rise,
> Age after age, than to arrest his course?
> All we behold is miracle." COWPER.

but I have ever had a keen relish for everything that was beautiful or curious in nature, and after my first visit hither I was impelled to come again simply by the extreme beauty of the fossils, as they appeared to my untutored eyes, and by a desire to take home the best I could find and place them where they would be better understood and more justly appreciated than they could be by myself. There was something striking to the imagination in finding not merely the impress where the leaf had been, nor even the leaf itself turned into something like the rock in which it was imbedded, but, to all appearance, the actual leaf itself, with every fibre and reticulation in its structure preserved as distinct and clear as when it grew, a living, organised structure. Many of the specimens were of a rich green hue and of a velvety surface, which made it difficult to remember that it was not the actual vegetable structure that we saw before us. Others were of a lustrous golden appearance, that would certainly have rendered it impossible to convince the good people of Sixt that we had not begun to work the gold mine they were afraid I had found. Then, again, there is no class of plants which seem to me to possess half the beauty of the fern-tribe, and it was an additional attraction to me to get this peep, at first hand, as it were, into the fern growth of an extinct period.

I went, therefore, as a simple lover of nature, having the time and the means to explore for myself a mine of hidden beauties, which it required no scientific or geological knowledge to enjoy and to be thankful for; and I entreat the reader to accept the present chapter as an attempt to portray the sort of life these expeditions involve, and the amusing incidents with which they abound, and perhaps to persuade him also to visit Moëd; and not as intended or expected to give any information as to the scientific character or geological history of the fossils which gave me so much pleasure. I brought a great number home, and at once offered to the authorities of the British Museum the first choice out of all my specimens. There was but one, which was remarkable for the number and variety of plants it contained, that I reserved for myself. It was with somewhat of a sorrowful feeling, I must confess it, that I found Mr. Woodward, the accomplished geologist whom they sent to look at them, pick out every single thing that I had set my heart upon keeping. He selected eighty specimens, and amongst them I certainly resigned every one that I had taken a particular fancy to. However, I thought

I had no business to keep for the gratification of my unlearned taste what might be put to a better use elsewhere, and I let them go without a murmur. I gave the next choice to my Alma Mater, University College, London; and Professor Morris, who has made this class of fossil plants his peculiar study, picked out two hundred more, which are now in the museum of the college. Professor Morris confirmed my impression of their singular beauty and perfectness, and told me he thought he could detect in some of them what was of extremely rare occurrence, distinct traces of the cellular structure preserved in the fossil leaf.

The fossil bed lay in a little ravine or gully, and consisted of a band of dark, schistaceous, slaty stone, varying from four or five to twenty or thirty feet in width, occupying a hollow between two beds of hard grey rock. The productive part of the band is about 300 feet from top to bottom; higher up, the grey stone closes in on either side, and the band nearly disappears, while lower down also it dwindles to very small dimensions, and is apparently quite unproductive. A few feet to the east I found a second band of slaty schist of less extent than the first; and farther still to the right another little watercourse descends nearly at right angles to the first, and its bed is of a similar substance. The second band, which, unlike the first, seems thrust up out of the grey stone instead of being overlapped by it, is also rich in fossil remains, principally, as we thought, ferns, but we had little time to investigate; and the third showed indications of vegetable fossils being not far off, but we had no time to find out exactly where.

All this time Bellin is at work at his mine, and when I have finished my rough sketch he is just ready to spring it. The operation is most successful, and detaches, amongst others, one magnificent slab, upwards of two feet long and full of beautiful remains, which is now in the British Museum. We begin eagerly to split up some of the other fragments, and find many new plants which we have not seen before. Amongst them appears the corner of something like a great gentian leaf. With infinite pains and anxiety (I could not help thinking more than once of Mrs. Todgers's remark to Mr. Pecksniff about the solicitudes of gravy), I chipped off all the superincumbent stratum and disclosed the entire specimen, eight inches long, and singularly perfect in all its details.

It is useless for me to attempt to describe all the beautiful leaves and plants we exhumed. The principal part of them were ferns, of which we found at least seven or eight distinct kinds; one of them so like our own *Osmunda regalis*, that it is difficult even now to believe what I am told, that it belongs to an extinct species; but we also found leaves like plantain leaves, petals like those of the most delicate and ragged pinks, blades of grass of several varieties, jointed stems decked with pointed fringes at each joint, just like our English mares' tails, slender whorls of bracts and stem-leaves which might almost be taken for flowers, and every here and there a large flattened branch of something like a bamboo, and what we took for the débris of coniferous trees. At every minute we seemed to find something either new or more beautiful than before. They have kept their colours and their fine markings well, and even now, when I turn to some that are at hand — with hopes and prospects so dashed and changed that I hardly know myself — the old enthusiasm returns, I feel the undying beauty of Nature, whether on her grandest or her minutest scale, whether she speaks to us of to-day or of ages long swept into the abyss of the past, and I could wish myself back again by the little watercourse of Moëd, doing stone-chipper's work under the scorching noonday sun.

We worked with right good will till one o'clock, when the time of day warned us, no less emphatically than our famishing insides, that we must dine, as we had a long afternoon's walk before us. We were almost reluctant to quit this interesting scene. Old Bellin, toiling for his few francs a day, was, if anything, the most excited of the party; but we were not provisioned for another night. So we put carefully aside on the turf all the best specimens for which we meant to send; and the few broken ones which contained something rare that we must have, we tied together and wrapped tenderly in paper; and then at length addressed ourselves to our homeward journey. Starting at half-past two, we descended the slopes of turf so rapidly, that by a quarter past three we had reached the Dioza. We did not go a mile or two round to take advantage of the only bridge across it, but sought and found a place where we could attain the opposite side by jumping from stone to stone.

This bank of the Dioza is excessively steep, and we fight our way up through sowthistles six feet high, and bracken nearly as tall, dally amidst the seductive charms of thousands of raspberry-bushes teeming with ripe and luscious fruit, and do not tear ourselves away till we are reminded by the already lengthening shadows that the sun sets early enough when the middle of September is past, and that we shall probably have to descend from Planpraz in the dark. The chalets of Arvelais, a little below the level of Moëd, are reached about half past four o'clock; and here, as Balmat and Bellin are heavily laden, and wish to stay awhile and drink some milk, I leave them, and wander gently on towards the wild gap in the chain of the Bréven, through which I have once passed before.

The common track (for a faint track has been worn even here by the feet of the shepherds and cow-herds) lies on the bare mountain side, exposed to the full power of the evening sun; but before long I hear the murmur of water, and find, a short distance out of the path, a ravine between the rocks, down which trickles a charming little stream of limpid water, breaking into a series of miniature cascades, with a clear little pool at the foot of each, every pebble at the bottom distinctly seen, though it be through several feet of water. The sides of the channel are overgrown with the richest tapestry of dark green moss I ever saw; and as I mount in the very bed of the stream, the trickling sound is so pleasant, and the shade so cool and refreshing, that I congratulate myself heartily on having found a line of ascent so much more beautiful and attractive than that I had taken before. These dark pools seem to be the death-places of many a grasshopper. They jump merrily from the sides and tumble into the cold water, get benumbed, and cannot extricate themselves. I saved five from a watery grave in one little pool alone. By and by, my ravine, like all things pleasant or painful, came to an end, and emerging into the full sunlight, I felt how much I had gained by the judicious choice of my path. The rest of the ascent is sufficiently toilsome, and on a snow-bed, near the top, we were very glad to stop and make some lemonade. I took advantage of the halt to make my toilette also, and washed, shaved, brushed my hair, and changed my poor old flannels, now hopelessly "abîmés" by the rough work at Moëd, for a pair of less way-worn greys.

It was nearly six o'clock when we reached the gap at the top of the ridge by which it is crossed. Whenever the mule-path, now contemplated between the Col d'Anterne and Chamouni, by way of the Bréven, shall be completed, this passage will, if I am not much mistaken, be looked upon as one of the great attractions of the excursion. The view is, to my taste, much finer than that from the summit above the Cheminée. You have the bold rocks of the Bréven on either hand, and Mont Blanc and the valley are framed as it were in a setting of broken crag. There is no other place I know from which so fine or so just a view of the Aiguille Verte can be obtained. You see the whole, or nearly the whole, of its western flank, and are able to appreciate its vast proportions. The Aiguille du Dru, which from most places near Chamouni seems close to it, and as high as, or higher than, the Aiguille Verte, here shrinks into its proper place and size. It appears, as it is in fact, separated from the Verte by a vast gap, and its loftier neighbour raises its glacier-crowned head some thousands of feet above it. Again we had a magnificent sunset; the rosy tints were just fading away as we descended upon Planpraz, and long before we reached Chamouni night had set in and the stars were shining brightly. I found I had quite forgotten my early dinner, and after a toilette supplementary to that of the snow-bed near the top of the Bréven, was quite ready for the evening table d'hôte.

SOME EXCURSIONS

AMONG

THE GREAT GLACIERS

CHAP. VIII.

"The most alluring clouds that mount the sky
Owe to a troubled element their forms."
WORDSWORTH.

" We climbed the mountain's height ;—
A storm came on, and we could see
No object higher than my knee.

'Twas mist and snow, and storm and snow,
No screen, no fence could we discover,
And then the wind ! in sooth it was
A wind full ten times over."
Ibid.

BAD WEATHER ON MONT BLANC.

POSSIBLE DANGERS OF BAD WEATHER.—BALMAT'S PROPOSED EXPERIMENT. — DR. TYNDALL'S ASSISTANCE. — OPPOSITION OF THE CHIEF GUIDE. — APPEAL TO THE INTENDANT. — GORGEOUS SUNSET AT THE GRANDS MULETS.—THE CORRIDOR.—THE MIST COMES ON.—SUMMIT OF MONT BLANC.—BURYING THE THERMOMETER.—INTENSE COLD.—APPEARANCE OF OUR PARTY. — BALMAT'S HANDS FROST-BITTEN. — HIS SUFFERINGS.— DESCENT OF THE MUR.—CONSIDERATION OF THE PORTERS. — SUDDEN CHANGE OF WEATHER. — STATE OF BALMAT'S HANDS.— FATE OF THE THERMOMETER.

MOST of us have, at some time or other in our lives, experienced the miseries which exposure to wind and weather is capable of inflicting. To ride half the night in drenching rain, or in a steady drizzle on an "outside car," in the wilds of Connemara, or over a pass amongst the English lakes, to buffet with the storm across a desolate Highland moor, to struggle in blinding snow through a strange and thinly inhabited country, are among the occasional necessities of most travellers — never free from abundant discomfort, not always from actual danger. Storm and wind have a specific effect of their own in lowering the vital powers and destroying the elements of resistance to their attacks. The case of the two gentlemen who perished on the well-marked path between King's House and Fort William, positively killed by bad weather on an August day*, though a striking, is far from being a solitary, instance of the death-dealing power which the elements can exert. But it is difficult, from the widest experience of bad weather at ordinary elevations, to form any conception of the terrible aspect it assumes on lofty mountains; where the fury of the blast is increased tenfold,—where rain gives place to snow,—where, perhaps, the very mist is frozen,—where the soil and rock are replaced

---

* In 1847. See Quarterly Review, vol. ci. p. 299.

by substances incapable of absorbing and of radiating heat, so that the instant the sun's rays are withdrawn, every source of warmth is extinguished, and where the scanty produce of caloric in the body is more than exhausted in raising the thin and frosty air you breathe to a temperature which the lungs can endure.

It has been my lot, among the many chances of an inveterate climber, to learn what bad weather means in a spot as lofty, and as remote from external assistance, as any in which I am likely, in Europe, at all events, again to incur the anger of the elements, namely, on the summit of Mont Blanc; and it was an experience such as the most reckless traveller would hardly soon forget, or willingly brave a second time. The circumstances of the expedition were peculiar. During the summer of 1857, Dr. Tyndall was engaged during some weeks in a series of researches on the Mer de Glace. Balmat mentioned to him that he thought of placing some self-registering thermometers on and near the summit of Mont Blanc, for the purpose of ascertaining the minimum of external temperature attained in that elevated region, and the depth to which such cold penetrates beneath the surface of the ice. Circumstances prevented Balmat from carrying out this experiment during the autumn of 1857; and, before the next campaign, Dr. Tyndall, believing that the result would be a valuable addition to our knowledge of the real phenomena and condition of the ice-world, procured from the Royal Society a small grant for the purpose of assisting so praiseworthy an undertaking. Proper thermometers were taken out from England; and, about the beginning of September, Dr. Tyndall repaired to Chamouni and proposed to Balmat to make the ascent and plant the thermometers. Balmat was at the time engaged as my guide, and I gladly accepted Dr. Tyndall's welcome invitation to be of the party. The weather, however, broke up, and, for some days, it seemed hopeless to think of any long or difficult expedition; and, despairing of Mont Blanc, we made a compromise by burying one thermometer in the ice and planting another beneath some rocks, above the summit of the Jardin. The depth of snow we encountered here appeared to afford satisfactory proof that it would be in vain to attempt Mont Blanc. The day, however, was one of singular magnificence, and the following day proving equally fine, we could none of us resist a longing desire to be once more amongst the grandest scenes of the ice-world, and to gain that glorious summit which rose so temptingly before our eyes. Balmat had another thermometer which, though not particularly suitable, would yet answer the purpose sufficiently well in default of a better. The expedition was therefore determined upon,—Balmat to be at its head, as the projector of the experiment,—Dr. Tyndall the scientific director, and prepared to make some interesting observations on other matters, — I to " make myself generally useful " as far as I could. We were met, however, by a not altogether unexpected difficulty. The then chief guide, a man entirely devoted to the old régime, declared that without the regulation number of guides, which means the regulation expense of about 25*l.* apiece, we should not go. We had each of us ample knowledge of Alpine climbing, had each of us ascended Mont Blanc before*, and were resolved that nothing should induce us to submit to this enormous imposition. We appealed to the superior authorities, to the Syndic, and through him to Monsieur de Bergoëns, the excellent and liberal Intendant of the province, and readily obtained from him an

---

* In 1857, Dr. Tyndall had performed the rare, and not very cautious, feat of ascending with one guide only ; and had, a few weeks before the time of the present expedition, climbed alone to the summit of Monte Rosa ; in my judgment, however, a much less arduous undertaking than his ascent of Mont Blanc.

official countenance for our proceedings, the result of which was that the chief guide's threats of prosecutions and procès-verbals were unheeded; and, instead of our having any difficulty in procuring the porters we required, we might have had a hundred if we had wanted them. Precious time, however,—two or three days of glorious weather,—had been lost in these negotiations, and when we started it was not altogether without a misgiving for the morrow.

The matchless grandeur of the scenery of Mont Blanc is neither generally known nor adequately appreciated: and, despite the great wasting of the glaciers, which was observable in the year 1858 in most parts of the Alps, the wonders of the ice-world of Mont Blanc were certainly greater than in the previous year. The difficulty of reaching the Grands Mulets was considerable, owing to the enormous magnitude of the crevasses beneath their base. One prodigious chasm stretched right across the Glacier de Taconnay, from the foot of the Grands Mulets to the summit of the Montagne de la Côte, and it was only after repeated trials and great delay that we found a practicable, though far from an easy passage. A wonderful but unpromising sunset closed the day, the sun sinking to rest amidst a chaos of gorgeous clouds, some piled and banked one upon another till they looked as solid as the rock on which we lay, others whirled in wild eddies by the rising west wind, or torn to rags and scattered piecemeal in space by some furious and transient blast, others floating calmly in loftier regions, looking down in quiet unconcern on the seething masses below, all lighted up in a thousand different tints by the glowing rays of the descending luminary: some crimson, some gold, some dark violet, some purple, some of the richest mixture of yellow and brown, some but faintly blushing, some scarcely differing in hue from the pale cold blue of the zenith sky, some even tinged with green. I thought of Heber's beautiful lines:—

> " I praised the sun, whose chariot rolled
> On wheels of amber and of gold;"

when lo! the central mass, behind which the sun was now nearly hidden, suddenly grew semitransparent, presenting an immeasurable depth of amber mist, itself apparently one vast reservoir of illuminating power. Quick as thought, disclosing still vaster deeps of space behind, a kind of tunnel opened through its very heart, out of which shot across the clear space in front a bright cone of ruddy light, which turned its own amber channel to a cylinder of melting gold, and lit up the dark forms of the mountains in the west with a strange unearthly glow. These gorgeous dioramas of celestial scenery seldom indicate settled weather; and it was not without misgivings that I watched a sunset scene which has been without a parallel in my recollection. The evening had not well closed in before a light fall of snow took place, followed by a storm of wind so furious that it seemed at times resolved to annihilate the little cabin which formed our shelter. The upper part of Mont Blanc was covered, through a great part of the night, with a dark misty cap, which experience taught us was but the whirlwind of dry snow that was eddying about the summit.

However, about one o'clock things looked better, the stars began to shine, and by half-past one we had started on our icy pilgrimage. The comet, which Dr. Tyndall and I had discovered the night before at the same instant, — I, certainly without having heard of it before, — was now blazing over the Col de Balme, and a considerable portion of the heaven was clear. The sky looked more and more promising as the night wore on; and when, half an hour before sunrise, we were on the Grand Plateau, and the air was cold and crisp and dry, we congratulated each other on the fair prospect of glorious weather at the top. A very great difficulty successfully overcome on the ascent of the Corridor raised our enthusiasm still higher; and it was only when we reached the summit of the Corridor, and exchanged the still and dry atmosphere of the northern side for a cold, misty, driving wind, charged with the moisture of a million clouds that lay in dense immovable masses over the whole sea of mountains to the south, through which but three solitary peaks — Monte Rosa, the Grand Combin, and the Matterhorn — were able to pierce, that we gave up our exalted hopes, and felt that we should be fortunate if we reached the summit without accident.

There was no time to be lost: we were already somewhat wearied with the deep snow, and a most fatiguing ascent still lay before us; so we stayed only to effect a more equitable division among our party of our one bottle of champagne than was practicable so long as the cork remained undrawn, and addressed ourselves seriously to the Mur de la Côte. We had not gone many hundred yards before a light drift of transparent mist, scarce enough to dim the rays of the sun, came dancing by us. It was but the precursor of many others;

and, from the time we reached the top of the Mur, we never saw the summit till we stood upon it. Still it was so clear upon the Chamouni side, the mist so often grew lighter and thinner, and the wind was so strong, that we could not help hoping it might partially, at any rate, clear off. When we were about half-way up the Calotte we caught our last glimpse of Chamouni, and our friends below had their last peep at us. We saw no sight or sign of the living world again till some four hours afterwards, when we emerged once more into sunshine and daylight on the Grand Plateau.

And now, as we fought our way up the steep Calotte, with beating hearts and panting lungs, the boiling mist eddied round us in denser and denser folds, the struggling beams of the watery sun grew fainter and fainter, the drifts of powdery snow, gathered by the south wind from the surface of the glacier, were swept more swiftly past us, though we purposely kept as much to the north and as far from the actual ridge as possible, for the sake of all the little shelter we could get. Suddenly, about half past nine o'clock, we found the steep incline at an end, and were welcomed by a sharp and eager blast as we stood once again on the summit of Mont Blanc. A site for the thermometer was soon selected, and, with the ice-hatchets and a long iron bar we had brought to mark the spot, our three stout young porters set vigorously to work to dig a hole three or four feet deep,—a cell in which the instrument should be immured till the genial suns of the next July or August should enable us, if the elements should spare it, to release the captive and extort the secrets of the icy prison-house. A mackintosh was thrown down on the snow, and a shelter against the wind constructed by stretching a plaid over some alpenstocks, where, two feet from the summit, Dr. Tyndall might boil some water and ascertain its temperature. A momentary lift in the fog was taken advantage of by Balmat and myself to creep some distance along the narrow ridge which forms the summit, to investigate the possibility of an ascent from the Grand Plateau by the Bosse de Dromédaire, a favourite project with Alpine explorers which at that time remained yet to be achieved. While we did so, the thick mist swooped down again upon us, and we seemed indeed alone, for we could neither see nor hear our companions.

Digging holes in the ice is not nearly so easy a task as it might be thought, and Balmat joined the efforts of his vigorous arm and determined will to those of our porters, who were all young men—from twenty to three and twenty years of age—and most of whom were making their first ascent. After watching Dr. Tyndall's fruitless efforts to get his lamp to light, in which most of our matches were already consumed, some of the drifting snow having got into the wick, I flung myself on a corner of his mackintosh, and endeavoured to reconcile myself to the misery of our situation. The thermometer, sheltered from the wind, stood at $-12\cdot3°$ Centigrade, or twenty-two degrees of Fahrenheit below the freezing point. What it was in the wind I had not the energy to determine, but it must have been considerably lower. Our party presented an odd aspect. Every man had tied his handkerchief over his hat to keep his ears from freezing; and Balmat and myself had linen masks covering the whole of the face below the eyes except the mouth and nostrils. Dr. Tyndall was more efficiently protected by a most useful beard and moustache. We were all blue in the face, and every hair was converted into a fine thread of ice.

It is commonly supposed that the summit of Mont Blanc presents a face of tremendous precipices towards the south. The extensive prevalence of this notion amongst even well-informed men, is a striking proof of what I have elsewhere ventured to assert, that, despite the number of ascents, and the multitude of accounts of them that have been given to the world, the exact character of the scenery and the topography of the mountain have been but imperfectly made known. Instead of the ridge of Mont Blanc ending abruptly in the precipices which overhang the Allée Blanche, it is separated from them by a broad stretch of undulating glacier, not less than a quarter of a mile wide. This was not an unimportant item in the forces arrayed against us; for, from the whole area of this snow-field, the dry and frozen snow on the surface was hurled in clouds against the summit, adding greatly to our difficulties and discomforts. At last, when we had endured for nearly a whole hour the combined attack of wind and mist and snow-drift, I began to get uneasy as to consequences. My hands and feet were almost without feeling, and one of Dr. Tyndall's feet was quite senseless; and on getting up from the snow, where a bursting headache had made me glad to lie as still as I could, I was so alarmed at the aspect of our party, that I called Dr. Tyndall's attention to it; and, abandoning all further attempts to boil water, we resolved instantly to depart. Our men looked like animated corpses; the livid hue of their faces had deepened almost into black; they were shrivelled and shrunk, and their features wore an expression of suffering and anxiety. Every hair, not only on our faces, but on the cloth or flannel of our coats, gaiters, or plaids, was an icicle. Dr. Tyndall's beard and moustache were white, scarcely a vestige of their proper colour being observable. He told me my eyelashes even were all coated with ice. The wind was howling round us, as if in an unholy triumph over our wretchedness. Balmat, I thought, looked particularly ill; but, with indefatigable zeal, he was still busy trampling down the snow into the hole where the thermometer now lay nearly four feet below the surface. The iron bar was sunk seven feet deep, leaving about three feet above the ice to guide those who might seek it the next autumn to the spot. I asked the men some questions, but every one seemed unwilling to open his mouth, and answered only with a gesture. "Let us be off at once," I exclaimed, "or we shall have some serious accident."

The words were hardly out of my mouth when Balmat came up to me and said quietly, "Je crains beaucoup que les mains me sont gelées," and on inquiry I then learned, for the first time, that an iron ladle, which I had provided for the purpose, had been forgotten at the Grands Mulets, and that he had actually scooped out the ice and snow from the hole with his hands! No wonder that a single pair of woollen gloves were not stout enough to resist the protracted action of such fearful cold. We gathered our traps together with all the haste we could, and in two minutes were out of sight of the summit, hurrying down the trackless waste of ice which forms the Calotte. We could not see thirty yards before us, and every trace of our ascending footsteps was completely obliterated; but, guided by the unerring sagacity of Balmat, we had no fear of losing the direction, even in that dreary mist. We had not gone many hundred yards, however, before Balmat again turned to me and said, " I feel a *something*. I think I shall look at my hands." And pulling off his gloves he found, to our horror, that, from the ends of the fingers to the knuckles, they were perfectly black. He said quietly, " There is no time to lose;" and, casting down his traps, began to rub his hands violently with the snow; then, as no trace of sensation appeared, he began to get alarmed, and begged us to beat his hands. " Frappez," he said, " frappez fortement; n'ayez pas peur; fortement, *fortement!*" So Dr. Tyndall took one hand, and I the other; and taking off our thick, heavy, fingerless gloves, used them to beat the black and senseless hands with all our might. In that thin atmosphere any exertion is severely felt, and at length I actually fell back upon the snow exhausted with the work, and was obliged to call upon one of our porters, all of whom seemed quite stupefied at the catastrophe, to relieve me. Then we rubbed him with brandy and gave him some rich cordial—a sort of liqueur that Dr. Tyndall had in his flask. All the while we were standing in the driving mist and pitiless wind, not a quarter of a mile from the summit of Mont Blanc.

At last, after about half an hour's incessant and violent labour, sensation began to return. I have witnessed some forms of acute suffering in my time, but such an exhibition of human agony I have never beheld, and I devoutly trust I never may again. He was at times quite unable to speak, and kept rubbing his hands in the snow and stamping about in a kind of frantic way, his quivering lips, bent brow, and dilated nostrils alone visible beneath the mask, and telling us what he was suffering. Then he would exclaim passionately, "Hélas! je souffre, je souffre." Then he would turn to us; and, with that generous devotion to others which marks a noble character, implore us not to expose ourselves on his account, and give us some directions as to the route. The painful excitement of the scene may be more easily imagined than described, and it was increased by our utter inability to do anything to help him. Every now and then he bit one or other of his fingers; and finding that, notwithstanding the torture which the rest caused him, these were still senseless, set to work again with redoubled vehemence to rub and beat the hand.

No less than three quarters of an hour were spent in this dreadful way, when he said it was not safe for us to stay longer, and we must move on. The porters took up the things he had dropped, and I carried his alpenstock, so that both hands were free to continue the rubbing, which he did with great energy. The descent of the Mur de la Côte was anxious work; for the mist was thick and the wind furious; and some of the loose snow, which had helped us greatly in the ascent, had been swept off, leaving us the hard and glassy ice beneath, on which to make our slippery way. However, it was safely accomplished; and a short distance down the Corridor we got out of the worst of the wind and the snow-drift, and found our foot-prints showing faintly on the otherwise trackless surface. It was at the top of the Corridor that I felt more than anywhere else the bewildering effect of the mist and the drift.

There is a wide, undulating snow-field, of very gentle inclination, and little to indicate the proper direction to be taken, and I saw how very easy it would be to go wrong. Our foot-prints once regained, we had of course no difficulty about the route. One tremendous chasm had to be passed on the middle of the Corridor, approached by a descent of thirty or forty feet down a bank of ice, whose inclination could not be less than 60°.*

It was touching to observe that Balmat was not one whit less thoughtful for the safety and comfort of every one else than when he was in the height of health and personal enjoyment. One of the porters, a young man named Édouard Bellin—who, if he lives, will be one of the most daring guides of Chamouni—could hardly keep the tears out of his eyes as he spoke to me of " Monsieur Balmat," whom he said he loved as much as his own father. Nor was it less touching to observe the eager anxiety of all these young men to spare him every sort of trouble or fatigue. From the Grands Mulets a

* I am perfectly aware how much steeper than is generally imagined a slope of 60° is; but the inclination of the Mur de la Côte is nearly 45°, and this was far steeper than the Mur. I remember that in places, without leaning back, I planted my hand in the snow behind me to keep myself from slipping, and that the feet of the person who followed me were just above my head.

great deal of baggage had to be carried, and our porters were over-weighted, but not one ounce would they let Balmat carry, and not one word of complaint or remark did we hear, at any time during the day, at the really severe labour imposed upon them. One remarkably handsome and intelligent young man, Joseph Favret, the son of the Syndic, not only carried an immense load, but afterwards encumbered himself with a heavy ladder we had left at the widest crevasse of the Glacier de Taconnay, and carried it a great distance to facilitate the descent of his comrades.

While we were descending the lower part of the Corridor it began to snow, and we made up our minds for bad weather. A very few minutes later, however, on reaching the level of the Grand Plateau, we experienced one of those marvellous, though not uncommon, vicissitudes of weather so characteristic of a mountain climate, and passed suddenly from an arctic to an almost tropical temperature. Mist and storm had passed away, as if by magic; and though the thick vapours were still circling round the higher parts of the mountain, a bright sun was shining upon us out of a blue and cloudless sky, and the broiling rays poured down upon our heads were shot back from the dazzling snow with such fierceness that the heat was almost unendurable. We learned afterwards that, from below, the Grand Plateau and the lower half of the Corridor had been visible most of the day; and persons unfamiliar with the climate of the higher Alps, had supposed it impossible that the light vapour they had seen hovering over the summit could cause us any serious inconvenience. Goldsmith's well-known simile is as destitute of physical truth as it is full of poetical beauty: —

> " As some tall cliff, that lifts its awful form,
> Swells from the vale and midway leaves the storm;
> Though round its breast the rolling clouds are spread,
> Eternal sunshine settles on its head."

We had not done with bad weather: when we left the Grands Mulets, a little before three o'clock, it was in a thick fall of snow, and it is not easy to imagine a more desolate and cheerless prospect than that of the cold dead white glacier and the naked rocks, backed by the falling snow, which effectually concealed all the distant portions of the prospect.

Poor Balmat's hands continued very painful all the way home, and sensation was but very imperfectly re-established in several fingers. The third finger of each hand was the worst. The back of each hand was swollen to a height of nearly an inch above the natural level, from the severe beating which had been administered. It was many weeks before they were entirely cured, and eventually several of the nails came off. He did not feel it prudent to accompany me over the Glacier du Tour, for which I started the next day, nor over the Col d'Erin, which I crossed three days later; but exactly a week after our Mont Blanc expedition I had the gratification of standing by his side on the next highest summit in Europe, the wonderful peak of Monte Rosa — nor did he suffer from the expedition.

Balmat was an old and honoured friend of mine long before this adventure; but, could anything have increased my regard for him, it would have been the manly fortitude with which he bore suffering about as severe as any the human frame can undergo, and the generous and affectionate care with which, in the midst of it all, he was constantly ministering to the wants or comforts of the rest of the party, and displaying the most thoughtful and scrupulous attention to every precaution by which accident might be prevented or danger averted. He told us that the pain he suffered was without a parallel in his experience, and that it was the pricking sensation every one has felt when the circulation is re-established after the hands or feet have been extremely cold, magnified a hundred-fold, and extending back through the arms and body till it seemed to centre in the heart. Nor was it for many hours that he could feel any kind of assurance that he would not lose some at least of his fingers. His first apprehension was, of course, that he might lose both hands. He had long had, however, a great notion of the interest, in a scientific point of view, of the experiment for which the expedition was undertaken; and his first thought had been that he could bear the calamity the better, as it had been met with in the cause of science. With a rare and unostentatious disinterestedness he at once made light of the suffering, the moment he felt that danger was at an end, and resolutely declined to receive the slightest remuneration for his services. He had originally thought of making the experiment himself, he said, and should have carried it out at his own cost; and, grateful as he was for the recognition by the Royal Society of its value, and to Dr. Tyndall for bringing it under their notice, he could not think of accepting anything for himself. The lecture-hall at Leeds rung with well-deserved applause when, shortly afterwards, at the meeting of the British Association, Dr. Tyndall recounted to the first *savans* of Europe, to most of whom Auguste Balmat is personally known, the danger he had undergone and the courage and disinterestedness he had displayed.

The thermometer was never recovered. Dr. Tyndall reascended, but sought for it in vain, in 1859, when he also placed at intervals in the ascent, and on the summit, a number of other thermometers. What will be their fate, it is impossible to predict with certainty; but, from the account which was given of the manner of placing them, at the meeting of the British Association at Aberdeen, in 1859, I should doubt very much if the higher ones will ever be recovered. I do not mean to imply that they might have been better planted. The difficulty is an intrinsic one. The wind has a force in those elevated regions which it is difficult to conceive without experience. It is said that when Napoleon Bonaparte was in possession of Savoy, he directed an iron cross to be fixed on the summit of Mont Blanc, and that this was done with every care to insure its durability; but that within four and twenty hours a storm arose and swept away every vestige of it. I may mention a very remarkable circumstance which Balmat told me with respect to the thermometer buried above the Jardin. He found the iron bar which marked its place, the following season, and the thermometer buried at its base; the thermometer was broken and therefore told little. The iron bar, which was as thick as a man's thumb, was bent nearly flat with the surface of the ice. That part of it which was buried in the ice was straight, although it was no longer perpendicular, but inclined forward at a considerable angle. It must have been the blows of the spring avalanches that bent the bar, and, considering the little surface of resistance it afforded for them to act upon, it gives a wonderful idea of the overwhelming velocity with which they glide down. The downward movement of the bar and the thermometer during the nine or ten months that they were buried was about 300 feet.

The chief guide did his best to bring our party to justice. He sent a spy off after us who might bear witness that we were all safe on the " Chemin du Mont Blanc." This fellow overtook us not far from the Pierre l'Échelle, and we had some difficulty in restraining our young porters from inflicting a little wholesome chastisement upon him. After our return, our whole party of guides and porters were summoned before the juge de paix at St. Gervais. The summons was served on Balmat one Tuesday afternoon, I think, to appear on the following Thursday. Balmat went off the next morning to the intendant at Bonneville. M. de Bergüens is not a man to be trifled with, and he considered it a piece of presumption on the part of the chief guide to institute this prosecution, after the Intendant had sanctioned our proceedings. He accordingly despatched the government advocate — I forget what he was called in those days — to St. Gervais to see that the judge was properly informed of all that had happened. That functionary travelled half the night to be at St. Gervais in time. The result was a great blow to the "party of obstruction." The summonses were dismissed, and the chief guide was packed off with "a flea in his ear." He was told that what was wanted for the wellbeing of Chamouni was "que les glaciers descenderaient un peu plus bas, et écraseraient quelques uns de ces gens si ignorants, si rétrogrades, afin que les autres pourraient marcher un peu mieux sans eux!" Whether this piece of eloquence came from the seat of justice, or only from the representative of the government, I forget, but it gave great satisfaction to the "party of progress." Our porters walked back in procession, with flowers in their hats, to Chamouni, and as they entered the village they caught sight of the unhappy chief guide; they pounced upon him, carried him to a neighbouring wine-shop, and inflicted upon him the ignominious punishment of making him hopelessly drunk, in which state they carried him through the streets in triumph.

CHAP. IX.

> " Far above,
> Where mortal footstep ne'er may hope to rove,
> Bare cliffs of rock, whose fixt, inherent dyes
> Rival the tints that float o'er summer skies;
> And the pure, glittering snow-realm, not so high,
> That seems a part of heaven's eternity."
>
> Mrs. Hemans.

THE COL D' ERIN.

THE GLACIER DU TOUR.—SION.—VAL D'ERIN.—CURIOUS PYRAMIDAL FORMATIONS. — EVOLENA. — UNPROMISING PROSPECTS.—A WALK IN THE DARK.—GLACIER DE FERPÉCLE.—ADVANCE OF THE GLACIER.—DIRT-BANDS. — CHALETS D'ABRICOLLA. — DANGEROUS PASSAGE. — THE MOTTA ROTTA.—THE COL.— STRIKING VIEW OF THE MATTERHORN.—MEASUREMENTS OF HEIGHT.—PASSING A BERGSCHRUND.—THE STOCKHI. — GLACIER OF ZMUTT. — REMARKABLE SOUNDS.—BEAUTIFUL DESCENT TO ZERMATT.

The day after the expedition recorded in the last chapter, my wife and I held council as to our next step. We had had no idea of moving on the very day after my ascent of Mont Blanc, but we were anxious to visit Monte Rosa, and we had been so delayed by the uncertain state of the weather that there was no time to lose, and after duly weighing pros and cons we determined to proceed at once. The weather was magnificent, just fit for "grandes courses," and my friend H. and myself were just in condition for them also, and it seemed to us all a pity that we should neglect so fair an opportunity for a grand excursion, by following the path I for one knew so well across the Tête Noire and the Forclaz. Balmat was quite ready to go forward, despite his accident, though it was not prudent for him to expose his injured hands again, just at present, to the glare of the sun reflected by the spotless glaciers, and he therefore *must* take the commonplace route if he went at all. My wife declared herself perfectly at ease under his care, besides which, a very dear and honoured friend of mine, the Vice-President of Queen's College, Cork, was going in the same direction with ourselves and kindly offered to take charge of her; so it was settled that she should stay at Chamouni till the following day, the 15th September, while H. and I should move up to the Col de Balme, and that on the evening of the 16th we should all rendezvous at Martigny, they by way of the Tête Noire, H. and I by the glaciers du Tour and d'Orny.

Our arrangements answered perfectly; the weather was propitious, each party had a delightful excursion, and each had a fund of pleasant anecdote for the other when we happily met, safe and sound, and nearly at the expected hour, at Martigny. *Our expedition had been most successful.* We had seen some phases of the ice-world new even to us who were not inexperienced ice-men. In particular we had descended in one place into the bosom of a crevasse, and had gazed upon a scene of fairy magnificence, of which it is difficult to give the most inadequate notion. We had found an arch of snow springing from the sides of the crevasse and meeting overhead, stretching away in either direction till it was lost in the mere obscurity of distance. As far as we could see on either hand, the translucent roof was hung with icicles two or three feet in length, as thick together as they could be planted, some hanging perpendicularly; others, where the block of half-ice-half-snow from which they were formed had sunk and altered its plane, inclining in one direction or the other and sometimes actually interlacing with contiguous groups, while here and there large clusters of them had fallen down and choked the crevasse with a bristling mass of débris.

In another part of the glacier we thread our way

through a suspicious maze of holes which give a honeycombed appearance to the glaciers. Impelled by curiosity one of us, after we have passed safely over, returns, and creeping on his hands and knees to the brink of one of the pitfalls, looks through, and finds to his horror and amazement that we have actually crossed an arched roof of ice springing from the sides of a crevasse not less than twenty feet in width, and of a depth so great that the imperfect light does not let him see to the bottom, and that at the spot on which he is kneeling — nearly the keystone of the arch — the cake of ice is less than a foot thick. An army might have been engulphed in it and no one been the wiser for it. We have also had the satisfaction of finding a new passage from the glacier du Tour to the glacier de Trient, far easier than the one by which W. and R. and I had descended the year before, and which is described in the volume of the Alpine Club.* Our friends had had a no less interesting day in the beautiful Tête Noire, and a more cheerful party seldom sat down to do justice to a well-earned meal

---

* " Peaks, Passes, and Glaciers," a series of Excursions by Members of the Alpine Club. Chap. i. " The Passage of the Fenêtre de Salena from the Col de Balme to the Val Ferret, by the Glacier du Tour, the Glacier de Trient, and the Glacier de Salena."

than the one which assembled round our table that evening at Martigny.

The next day we made but a short journey of it, taking carriage to Sion and stopping there. We all enjoyed the afternoon's rest, and again held a council of war, when it was determined that we should once more separate for a day and a half, that H. and I should avail ourselves of the still glorious weather to cross the Col d'Erin, which we had long been anxious to undertake, and that my wife should move on quietly to Visp, sleep there, and make her way the following day by the usual route to Zermatt. We had brought with us, besides Balmat, another old friend, François Cachat, and stout young Édouard Bellin, who had accompanied us as porter over the Col du Tour and the Glacier d'Orny, had begged permission to go on with us, as he wished to see Monte Rosa and the neighbourhood. Balmat was very reluctant to forego a " grande course," but either he or I must give it up, as I trusted the care of my wife to no one else; so he went with Madame by the valleys, and the Col d'Erin party consisted of H., myself, Cachat, and Bellin.

About half-past six the next morning we parted, H. and I. making across the plain of the Rhône for the valley which opens out of it to the south, just opposite to Sion, and the rest taking carriage for Visp. The walk up the Val d'Erin to Evolena is one of singular richness and luxuriant beauty, but the mountain ranges are very close on either hand and there is but little distant prospect. It should be traversed early in the day—we were much too late —for the heat is perfectly awful. The valley of St. Nicholas is hot enough on a close August day, but I have never felt anything elsewhere that came near to the sultriness of the Val d'Erin on this 17th of September. It was so great that our sense of the extreme beauty of the vegetation, and of the smiling character of the scenery, has been almost obliterated by the recollection of thirst and weariness; and we arrived at Evolena quite tired down, though it was but about two o'clock when we reached it.

I must not omit to mention one very singular feature of the scenery in the lower part of the valley. The torrents have in many places cut away the soil in the most singular fashion, leaving great pyramidal wedges, varying in height perhaps from 40 or 50 to 200 feet, or even more, standing edgeways towards the valley, with deep ravines between them. They often rise into sharp needle-like peaks, and on the tops of many of them are perched large bosses of turf, the remnants of the surface of the mountain

SINGULAR FORMATIONS. 253

before the intervening spaces were torn open by the water. The effect is most singular. From a distance the bosses of turf look like masses of rock, and each pyramid so crowned seems a little Peter Botte mountain. We could not imagine how blocks of stone could be so lodged, but it was not till we were close to them that we discovered that the supposed rocks were bits of turf, and were able to fathom the mystery.

PYRAMIDS OF EARTH IN THE VAL D'ENIN.

We had been led to suppose that we should find capital quarters at Evolena. A new hotel, it was said, was just finished, which would offer excellent accommodation to the wayfarer; and on approaching the village, which stands in a little elevated plain strewn with boulders and débris, we had noticed a large and handsome building which we supposed must be the hostelry in question. On coming closer, however, we saw that it was only half finished, and we could not find a single person about it. The village seemed nearly empty, and our appearance did not excite the least curiosity. After a great deal of difficulty the landlord was hunted up, but he said he had nothing ready and did not "receive" at present, though next season he would have twenty beds disposable. He struck us as a man of sanguine temperament to build a large hotel in a place where not a score of travellers pass from one summer's end to another. We persuaded him to do his best for us, and a couple of beds were soon rigged up and looked comfortable enough. But we wanted something besides beds, for we had walked seven hours in a broiling sun, and our recollections of breakfast were very shadowy. Our host manifested a lordly indifference to our wants, shrugged his shoulders, and said he did not know what the village could furnish except black bread and the salted mutton of last year; not a very promising prospect for four hungry travellers. We were obliged to make the best of what we could get. Our host remembered at last that he had shot a partridge himself, and was keeping it for Sunday's dinner, and this he now generously abandoned to us. The cooking was as dilatory as the fare was scanty, and it was nearly five o'clock before we got our "dinner," as it was euphemistically termed. The salt mutton was so hard and so salt that it beat H. and myself, and we had to content ourselves with half a partridge apiece, and some soup which looked and tasted like diluted dish-water. We ate as much bread and cheese as we could, but there was only one small piece of anything but the black bread to be had; and, to people who are not used to it, there is something exceedingly unpleasant in the sodden unwholesome taste of the black bread.

The clouds had gathered in the afternoon, and before nightfall it was mizzling fast, and things looked very bad for the long pass of the Col d'Erin. However, we resolved to have everything ready, and as Cachat seemed more shy than we had expected of attempting to find the passage for ourselves, we engaged a peasant of this valley to take us to the top of the pass, whence we thought we surely could accomplish the descent by ourselves. Our next care was to secure something in the way of food to take with us. We had been solemnly assured that there were no fowls to be had; but one unlucky wight was fool enough to crow, and finding that he belonged to our landlord, we put on moral pressure sufficient to make him, at all events, find his way into our bag — and we soon heard the poor fellow's last scream as the sacrifice was being consummated. Our landlord did not so much mind, it appeared, parting with this particular bird, inasmuch as he was an aged cock, past being of much use in the farm-yard. The hens we could not prevail upon him to sell us at any price; but he let us have a dozen eggs.

These preparations made, we betook ourselves to bed, with only faint hopes of being able to push across the Col on the next day. I was determined to do it, if possible, for I did not want my wife to be left alone at Zermatt, perhaps in anxiety about us; and I was much relieved when Cachat called us about half past one on the 18th, and told us the weather had so far improved that he thought we might venture to start. Our beds were so much better than our fare had been that we were positively reluctant to quit them, but we knew we had a long day before us, and we were soon dressed, and found a meal, far better than our supper of last night, awaiting us; for we had tolerable coffee, excellent milk, butter, and honey, and some very sour whity-brown bread, warmed on one side and called toast. Our host was an astute man; for, when I asked what there was to pay, he answered, ten francs for the provisions we were to take with us — "the cock," he said, "the eggs and the wine, and" (comprehensive phrase!) "tout cela," and for the rest, as we had been badly lodged, and he did not yet keep an inn, "à volonté." He had us in a cleft stick, for we did not like to chaffer with a man who had put himself to inconvenience to receive us; and, supposing that our men had taken wine with them from here, we paid the ten francs without question or demur, and offered him fifteen francs for the night's accommodation and the food we had eaten, with which he seemed by no means content, and we made it up to eighteen francs. Alack! by and by we found there was no wine in the knapsacks, save our own one bottle of champagne, brought from Sion, and that our ten francs had purchased nothing but an old and wiry rooster, a dozen hard-boiled eggs, and a small quantity of cheese and black bread! I fancy our host will manage to make the few travellers he gets pay for his expensive building, somehow or another.

Having made the best we could of our black-bread breakfast, we filed off at half past two, by no means sorry to quit such very bad quarters, even though it would take us many an hour to reach any better. With the Evolena man, we were five in all. There was no moonlight, and at this time but very little starlight, and we had therefore to depend upon the light of a lantern, carried by our Evolena friend. The path for some distance beyond Evolena is excellent. It is only when it approaches the habitations of man, and brings us to some group of chalets, that it becomes bad; and then, in order to enable passengers to avoid the mud and filth which always accumulate about chalets, large blocks of stone are cast in the path, to raise the feet above the miry slough, and the footing is rough, broken, and uncertain. There is something very solemn in these midnight expeditions: a party of resolute men, armed with the engines of mountain warfare, stealing noiselessly along through the hours of darkness, picking, or rather groping, their way through narrow passages, by the side of mountain torrents, or across the upland pastures, as if to surprise the Spirit of the glaciers before he is up and abroad. The utter impossibility of judging of distances, rendered, if that could be, more hopeless still by the bright gleams of flickering light flung from the lantern across your path, and bewildering your eye—the dark forms of neighbouring mountains, apparently so close upon you that they may be touched—the brawling of the distant, though now unseen, torrent—the steady, quiet, determined pace of your party, all combine to produce an effect upon the imagination which one would be sorry not to have experienced. Then, the deep silence of the sleeping hamlets through which you pass makes you feel as if you were amongst the habitations of the dead. Very often, you see some mysterious object towering through the darkness, and cannot tell what it is, till an accidental ray of light falls upon it, and shows it to be a chalet close at hand, while you have imagined it some distant wall of precipices. I remember once this night being fairly startled, a little way beyond the village of Haudères; I was walking steadily on, in front of the lantern, my eyes bent upon the ground to enable me to pick my way over the stones, when, looking up, I saw a great moving figure coming down directly upon me. It took me more than a moment to recognise my own shadow upon the side of a chalet which projected into the middle of our track. It is always much the most comfortable plan to go in front of the lantern. If it is before you, the constant endeavour to see the ground, in spite of the brilliant point of light just beyond it, is most fatiguing; whereas, by walking in front, you get a much more subdued and general light, and are freed from the embarrassing effect of a point of illumination shining just into your eyes.

It is surprising how long before daybreak there is some faint gleam of light shed over the face of the earth. The sun does not rise, at the time of the year of which I am speaking, till nearly six o'clock. Daylight would scarcely be acknowledged as even beginning before five, yet in this valley, which runs north and south, and from which therefore the earliest rays are blocked out, instead of its being enfiladed by them, I found it quite light enough to walk without the lantern at four o'clock. The moment you can do so, it is far more pleasant to dispense with artificial light, for the faintest general illumination is better than the partial and uncertain light thrown by a moving lantern, which intensifies actual shades and magnifies apparent lights, so as to distort the face of the ground, and throw the most wary of travellers off his guard as to the real magnitude of obstacles in his path. Accordingly, I got well ahead of the lantern wherever I could, and by four o'clock found myself entirely independent of its aid. I could then get a good way on in front, and turning round could enjoy the picturesque appearance of the rest of our little party, dimly seen by the dancing light.

Soon after passing Haudères, I thought I perceived an unusual foliage on the trees, and gathering a leaf as I passed, was surprised to find, on the lantern coming up, that it belonged to a plane-tree. I remembered, then, that Professor Forbes mentions plane-trees as growing here. They appeared to me, as well as the darkness would let me judge, to be in great abundance, and to grow to a considerable size. The trunks of some of them must have been two feet in diameter. The barberry I could distinguish as flourishing freely, and, in one place, a bush, which had looked in the dark like something uncommon, turned out to be a wild rose-tree; so that this part of the valley is not destitute of a beautiful growth of trees and underwood.

We had now got well past the opening of a wide valley on our right, which leads to the Col de Collon, and by that passage to the Val Biona and Aosta, and were steadily working our way up the left-hand valley, belonging to the stream of the Ferpêcle glacier. The path is carried high above the stream, and has to make some considerable détours to cross ravines which come down on the left, and contribute their quota to the great flood roaring in the dark depth below. In one place, which we reached just as the light was getting strong enough to make walking quite agreeable, the bed of the stream is contracted to a narrow gorge, through which the river foams and thunders far below; the path is carried over some rocks just overhanging the gloomy abyss, and in the dark it would be easy enough to step over the edge into no uncertain destruction. At this point the foot of the glacier first came into sight, creeping down towards the valley, at no great distance from us, though how far exactly, it was not yet light enough to discern. A little way further we crossed an immense mass of débris, which appeared to have come down from the rocks on the opposite side of the stream, and to have been scattered by the violence of the fall, to some height above us, along the gentler slopes on our left; for on this side there was no appearance of any such disruption having taken place, and the only precipices from which rocks might have rolled lay too far back to have given rise to the phenomenon.

It grew rapidly lighter as we crossed this stony waste, and a few minutes more brought us to two or three dirty chalets, where our Evolena friend left his lantern. It was now nearly five o'clock, and the tints of early dawn had made themselves unmistakeably visible. The weather did not look bad. From the moment we started the north wind had been struggling for the mastery, and had in part succeeded. He had rolled back from time to time the curtain of clouds, and revealed the stars shining brightly from his own quarter of the heavens. Not being able to see much on the earth, I had been watching the sky keenly, and was much surprised, as early as half past four, to notice a delicate amber tint, a real piece of *colour*, steal over some of the eastern and southern clouds. It was transient, but I am certain I was not deceived.

We now began to approach very near to the glacier, but we could as yet see little of the upper portion, over which our route lay. We saw a long dirty tongue of highly compressed glacier extending towards us, and over this a precipitous rock nearly in front of us, with some ice-precipices above it— the Motta Rotta — and to the right, a long serrated ridge, the Mont Miné, which divides the glacier into two portions, and runs far up into its basin. Further still to the right was a fine range of snowy peaks— the Aiguilles de la Za — portions of the western boundary of the great Glacier of Ferpêcle; but of the mass of the glacier itself we saw little or nothing.

We soon found that the path lay, not over the glacier, but by its side, among a waste of boulders covered with moss, interspersed with the stumps of dead pines and with living larches, and ornamented with a strong undergrowth of rhododendron. Formerly, our Evolena man told us, the track lay on the moraine of the glacier; but in 1852 the glacier increased so much as to destroy the old path, and since then people have always passed higher up along the eastern bank—by a far pleasanter path, I should say, than over the moraine. I asked him if the glacier had diminished that year (1858). He said, a little perhaps; but it does not seem to have exhibited the remarkable diminution that had been shown by every other glacier I had visited in the course of that journey. After passing for nearly an hour along what I have called the eastern bank of the glacier, but what is in reality to all appearance an ancient moraine, we had to take to a steep and lofty mountain covered with rough turf, and broken here and there into precipitous faces of rock, and to climb to a great height in order to gain the upper plateau of the glacier. In so doing we were rewarded by magnificent views of the glacier, and of the peaks and ranges round about it.

The glacier of Ferpêcle is one of the largest I have seen in Switzerland. It appears to me to be larger than the Fée, but it is certainly not so fine as that singularly interesting glacier. It is divided into two great branches by the chain of the Mont Miné, which extends nearly from the lower end of the ice-stream to the Tête Blanche, a point in the lofty range dividing the glacier of Ferpêcle from that of Zmutt. The smaller arm is the eastern, up which we were to make our way. The larger, and probably the finer, is the western, enclosed between the chain of the Mont Miné on the east, and the more important chain of the Aiguilles de la Za and the Dent de Bérauk on the west—that chain which is prolonged towards Haudères, and along whose western flank the path to the Col de Collon is carried. The upper part, the névé portion, of this western arm is only partly seen, being hidden to a great extent by the dark serrated line of the Mont Miné; but a fine ice-fall, in the nature of that of the Col du Géant, though neither so lofty nor so precipitous, is in full view. Beneath it, as beneath the ice-cataract of the Géant, the ice is very compact, and its surface wrinkled into numerous folds. Below these folds the dirt-bands begin. So many of them are double, or else they are separated from one another by so short an interval, that it is difficult to estimate their number with any precision; but, counting them as accurately as I could, I numbered no less than forty-three. They begin by lying nearly straight across the glacier, and stretch out at length into elongated curves. The dip of the lower curves was beautifully marked against the steep side of the glacier, where they striped it like so many dark bars, each falling more forward than its predecessor; thus:—

It struck me that there was a great deal to be learned from an attentive examination of the glacier of Ferpêcle, especially with regard to the dirt-bands. My opportunities of observation were limited to the distant view I had from the bank, but I was unable to see any dirt-bands peculiar to the eastern branch.

They are first exhibited on the western branch, just below the ice-cascade. Lower down, however, they are strongly developed right across the glacier; and the manner in which, as portrayed above, they run down the face of its eastern side, and display a continually increasing " frontal dip," is calculated strongly to impress the mind with the notion that they are connected, in some way, with the veined structure. But unless the motion of the Glacier de Ferpêcle be much slower than that of any great glacier whose motion has been measured, their close proximity to one another would seem almost fatal to the supposition that there is any connection between their intervals and the annual amount of motion of the glacier. But, as I have ventured elsewhere to remark*, it seems to me that we do not yet know the first facts necessary to be determined before we can construct a satisfactory theory of dirt-bands. " We do not know what is the contour of the glacier in early spring; whether its ridges and hollows exist along its whole length, or only beneath some tremendous ice-fall; whether the dirt-bands are constant in number, and are found at the same time of the year in the same part of the glacier. Indeed, we

---

* National Review for July, 1859, p. 27.

know very little about them except that they afford a graphic and lively illustration of the semi-fluid character, on the large scale, of glacier motion."

One portion of the glacier, as I have mentioned, descends from the left, where the upper part is a wide basin enclosed between the precipices of a very lofty and pointed peak called the Dent Blanche on the left and the Mont Miné range on the right. The whole of this expanse, several miles across in its upper portions, is filled by the glacier. It is broken, near the centre of the amphitheatre, by the fine precipitous mass of black rock I have mentioned before as the Motta Rotta, which is crowned by a lofty wall of ice, but upon whose steep face scarcely a snow-fleck rests. Beneath the Motta Rotta the glacier is much crevassed; but once on a level with it, so far as we could judge, little was to be met with besides enormous fields of unbroken snow. We were not yet, however, on a level with the Motta Rotta, and it was not easy to say with certainty what might be the real nature of the fore-shortened landscape on which we were looking.

The Col lies far away to the right, near to the extremity of the Mont Miné range, and it would certainly save a good hour or two if it were practicable to pass to the right of the Mont Miné. But the passage of the Col d'Erin is not yet well known, and the few persons who have made it have all passed to the left, and we followed the general practice. Leaving two wretched huts, the Chalets d'Abricolla, where travellers have been wild enough to pass the night, which we had reached after an hour's climb from the moraine, we worked our way for upwards of another hour across one of the vastest collections of stony débris I have ever seen. We were now getting beneath the offshoots of the Dent Blanche, the chief contributors to this prodigious waste of dreary ruins, and small glaciers every now and then overhung our path most unpleasantly. I should call this portion of the passage dangerous. The huge accumulation of stones has been partly brought together by the water-courses; but every here and there you pass over portions which have a different aspect, and contain rocks of much greater size, containing a large intermixture of stones and boulders that have travelled from the loftiest heights. At such a spot, if you look up, you are sure to see the end of a dirty glacier peeping over the edge of the heap of débris, as if watching your progress. You will probably see also that it is charged with a number of huge stones, just tottering on its brink. If in the humour to dispute your passage, it may cause you no small risk and alarm, if not a serious injury, by hurling one or two of them upon your head as you pass beneath. We escaped such a salute, but had hardly passed when a very large boulder came leaping down across our track, bounding fifty and a hundred feet at a leap, as if to remind us that we were there on sufferance only.

We came at length to a genuine lateral moraine, after climbing which for many minutes we arrived, just after seven o'clock, on the edge of the upper part of the Ferpêcle Glacier. The weather was looking very bad again; upon the chain of the Diablerets, to the north, it had been raining heavily for nearly an hour, and now the rain was falling fast upon the mountains bounding the Val d'Erin on the west, and dense masses of mist were rolling up the valley before the north wind. The grand white peak and shaggy side of the Dent Blanche, which had been towering, apparently to an immeasurable height, upon our left, were already shrouded in mist, and only casual and occasional peeps could be had, in which the grandeur of the scene was, if possible, enhanced by the mysterious way in which peak and precipice, rock and snow, appeared and disappeared, not among terrestrial objects, but high above our heads amongst cloud and sky. We could still see the precipices of the Motta Rotta, which formed a useful landmark to direct our course.

For the present, however, we did not much need a landmark, for some persons had made the passage two days before, and their track was well-marked from the place where we struck the glacier. After about twenty minutes' rest, and a meal of bread and cheese and champagne, we betook ourselves to the ice, and, following the footsteps of our predecessors, pushed straight towards the Motta Rotta. Having cut through one or two systems of formidable crevasses, transverse to the axes of converging wedges of glacier, we turned to the left and made for the precipices of the Dent Blanche. One of these, under which we had to pass, presented a quaint appearance. It was a black convex face of perpendicular rock, capped with a dome of snow, which reminded me of the rounded head of a shark rising out of the water to seize his prey. The resemblance was enhanced by a boss of rock thrusting itself out through the snow, just where the shark's eye should be.

The reason for our taking this course was soon visible; for it appeared that the portion of the glacier we were approaching is raised on a high terrace of rock, and that it was only by gaining the extremity of the wall of crag on the left, where it begins and is of insignificant dimensions, that we could pass from the lower to the upper section of the glacier. Having done so, we could again take our proper direction, bearing to the right, and proceed nearly in a straight line towards the Col, which lay far away, nearly south of the Motta Rotta, just below a small peak called the Tête Blanche, which is seen from some parts of the Val d'Erin, but not, if I remember right, from the ascent to the glacier.

From this point we scarcely met with a single crevasse; we kept pretty high up on the glacier, skirting its south-eastern boundary, a long irregular line of snowy swells and domes rather than of peaks, and leaving the Dent Blanche on our left and behind us. For two hours there was scarcely anything to diversify the route or attract the attention. New snow had fallen the night before, and had all but obliterated the footprints of our predecessors, so that the walking was very laborious. The glacier was seldom steep, except in one spot, just as we were coasting the upper edge of the Motta Rotta, where there were a few minutes of ascent worthy of Mont Blanc himself. The heat was intense;

the sun's rays penetrated through the mist without dispersing it, and made us feel as if we were in a vapour bath. This part of the route must be very fine when the atmosphere is clear. Over the Mont Miné range rise the loftier peaks of the western boundary of the glacier — all partaking of the same general pyramidal character in which nature seems to rejoice in this part of the Alps; all of very dark rock, sufficiently broken to permit the deposit of a beautiful network of snow. To the north lies the rich valley of Evolena, opening to the spectator one glimpse of the wider valley of the Rhône, and of the chain of the Diablerets and the Sanetsch beyond. When there is leisure to turn round, the Dent Blanche, one of the finest peaks in the Alps, rises suddenly and sharply almost from your feet far into the sky.

We, however, had very little view beyond an occasional glimpse of the valley of Evolena, till we neared the summit of the Col, when the clouds began to disperse, and we saw the head of the Mont Miné chain, now dwarfed into inconsiderable rocks, peeping out of the snow, and in front of them the portion of the glacier which passes beneath the western side of the Motta Rotta, sweeping majestically down, intersected by wide and deep crevasses, and occasionally breaking into séraques which would have done no discredit to the Glacier du Géant. The ridge on our left was sinking rapidly towards a depression, beyond which it rose again in the peak of the Tête Blanche. Through this depression it was evident we were to pass. Fortunately for the effect of the scene, you can see scarcely anything of what lies beyond the Col till within a very few paces of it. Those few paces are sufficient to disclose, in a few moments, a scene of novel character and of unsurpassed magnificence.

The long low wall of snow close on our left was suddenly replaced by no less wonderful an object than the peak of the Matterhorn itself, not six miles distant from the spot on which we stood, and still between three and four thousand feet above us, presenting to our astonished gaze a sheer precipice of nearly seven thousand feet from the summit to the glacier of Zmutt below; the strata in many places so quaintly twisted and contorted as to strike the eye at once on beholding it, and to suggest the thought what awful convulsions must have been Nature's birth-throes when this gigantic object was produced. It is impossible to convey any idea of the imposing aspect of the Matterhorn as beheld from this point. As seen from Zermatt and from all the more usual points of view, the mountain presents itself edgeways rather than sideways, so that you look directly, not upon a face of rock, but upon a sharp *arête*, sloping down towards you, with immense precipices on either side; but here we were face to face with one of these precipitous walls, and perceived for the first time its real height and steepness. I doubt if anywhere else in Europe such a precipice is to be seen. For thousands of feet together, it is too steep to be able to retain any but the lightest and most scattered deposit of snow; and as the eye ranges over its rugged surface, the huge mass tapers, now gently, now abruptly, till it ends in a narrow blunted ridge of rock, far up in the blue sky, yet so near as to be seen with wonderful distinctness. Nor is this great peak an object of solitary grandeur. Considerably nearer to our Col —in fact, just opposite the opening—is the Dent d'Erin, not a thousand feet lower than the Matterhorn itself, and ending in a huge system of precipices equally abrupt and inaccessible with those of its more gigantic neighbour. Its inferior elevation and the greater height of the glaciers out of which it springs alone detract from its comparative magnificence. It has a sharper and more graceful outline; its precipices are still more abrupt, though not so profound; there are purer and whiter snows about the base of its pinnacle; and beneath its faces of rock a beautiful curtain of glacier, so steep as to give one the impression of a precipice of ice, connects it with the glacier of Zmutt. It is connected also with the Matterhorn, by one long unbroken sweep of rock, sometimes bare, sometimes clothed with a similar graceful curtain of ice, steeper and loftier than any other I remember to have seen. Looking at these remarkable masses of ice, you get some little notion of how steep the faces of rock must be on which neither ice nor snow can lie, when you see ice lying for some fifteen hundred feet together in a bank so like a precipice as this.

I have never met with a scene so difficult to describe. It is so grand and so vast, and yet so simple, that when you have said that the Matterhorn and the Dent d'Erin are before you — stupendous precipices of rock and snow — you have almost said all that is to be said of the salient objects in the prospect. Yet in all my Alpine wanderings I have never seen a prospect which seemed to me quite so full of majesty as this.

The Dent d'Erin springs from a very lofty system of glaciers which sweep round from its base to the Col d'Erin and occupy the right-hand portion of the view. They rise gently as they retire, till they reach a height of several hundreds of feet above the Col. Immediately in front is the glacier of Zmutt, but on a much lower level than that on which we stand, and separated from the glacier of Ferpêcle by abrupt faces of black crag. It gradually rises towards the ridge between the Dent d'Erin and the Tête Blanche, where one common snowfield unites it with the highest portion of the glacier of Ferpêcle. As if forgetful of its community of origin, it has now separated itself far enough from the Ferpêcle Glacier, and leaves the traveller to get from the higher to the lower level as best he may. The difference of level is only two or three hundred feet, but the terrace on which the glacier of Ferpêcle is reared is excessively steep. It consists partly of rock, partly of a curtain of glacier such as is always found at the junction of a glacier, in the region of the névé, with a face of rock; and, according also to universal rule, this curtain is separated from the mass of the glacier below by a great crevasse or bergschrund, which commences almost as soon as the cliffs begin, and runs along nearly the whole subsequent length of the glacier.

Beyond the bergschrund lay our descending route; we had to travel down the glacier for some distance, and then, working our way across it, to reach some rocks (called by Professor Forbes the Stöckhi, in Studer's map, the Stockhorn), protruding on this side but a short distance from the snow, but beneath which, on the further side, we could see that a second arm of the glacier lay at a great depth.

I boiled water at Evolena before starting, and again on the summit of the Col, and, as I thought, made each observation with all the care I could; but the result I got is so exceptional, so seriously at variance with several recorded measurements before me, that I can have no doubt that my own observations are in fault, and I therefore forbear to give them. Professor Forbes estimates the height of an eminence in the ridge a good deal loftier than the Col at 11,760 English feet; but I have no idea of the height of the point in question above the Col, and therefore cannot deduce thence what would be his measurement of the Col itself; a barometrical measurement by MM. G. Studer and Ulrich, from observations made on the 15th August, 1849, gives 11,203 French, or 11,939 English feet; and boiling-water observations, for which I am indebted to Mr. F. F. Tuckett, of Bristol, made on the 20th June, 1856, give 11,612

English feet. I am inclined to think the estimation of MM. Studer and Ulrich is too high. There are very few passes in the Alps which attain anything like 12,000 feet. I was indebted to the courtesy of M. Plantamour, of the Observatory at Geneva, for a list of barometrical readings at Geneva, and at the St. Bernard, simultaneous with my own observations throughout this journey; so that I was able to test the results of my experiments by comparison of those obtained by working from the readings at each place with which he kindly furnished me, and I am satisfied that the error was in the observation at the top of the Col, and not in that at Evolena; but I cannot discover to what cause it was due.

We had reached the Col, after nearly nine hours' walking, soon after eleven o'clock. We had not come quite so quickly as we had hoped, on account of H., who was seriously unwell. The heat of the previous day, the long fast, and the bad food at Evolena, had completely upset him, and it was no little relief to us all to have him safely at the summit, with hardly another ascending step before him. We made a short halt on the Col, where we lunched and dismissed our Evolena guide. The wretched living of the valley did not seem to have agreed very well with him; he was utterly unfit for hard work, and for the last three hours had been unable to take his place in front, to make the steps in the snow, when his turn came.

We left the Col at half-past eleven, and turning very sharp to the left began our descent by passing diagonally down a snow-slope, just under the low ridge we had skirted so long before we reached the Col. Here we saw one of the most wonderful sights the ice-world can offer. The upper part of the snow-slope consisted of five successive beds of snow piled one on the top of the other, each overhanging the one beneath, and each fringed with a thick border of long ice-pendants. Picture to yourself this scene sparkling in a mid-day sun. Can anything be imagined more fantastically beautiful? — the soft white snow-bank curling over as it rose gently from the northern side of the ridge, and breaking into a surge of icicles, bound together at their bases by a thick incrustation of fresh-fallen snow — this wintery fringe repeated in five successive terraces, till the lowest ones were fairly in the shade of the upper — and we passed so close beneath the overhanging mass that my shoulder brushed off some of the icicles.

Just underneath this spot we scrambled down some rocks, and working diagonally downwards approached the bergschrund. We were all four tied together. The bergschrund was arched over with soft snow. Bellin was first, I second, H. third, and Cachat brought up the rear. Bellin slid over the bridge. He had not waited for H., who was third, to come close enough to him, and H. misunderstood something that Cachat said, and shortened my rope instead of slackening it. The consequence was that I was thrown down on my face in the middle of the snow-bridge, and was detained there for some seconds. Each of my arms went through in one place, and one of my knees in another, and I saw that the crevasse was seven or eight feet wide, and of great depth. I knew that if I did not lie still I should go through, and so I kept perfectly quiet till the misapprehension was removed. H. gave me rope enough, and Bellin hauled me across, after which H. and Cachat, each in his turn, lay down at full length, and were drawn across in the same way, and we all stood safe below this formidable obstacle.

We now worked rapidly down to the Stöckhi. There is perhaps nothing in Alpine travelling, especially amongst the higher glaciers, so surprising, nothing which is so ever new, as the effect upon the view of change of position. Features of the scene which looked a while ago absolutely contiguous, turn out to be separated by great chasms and valleys, domes turn into ridges, ridges into precipices, and grand magic transformations are enacted at every moment. Nowhere have I seen a better illustration of this fact than on the short descent to the Stöckhi. From the Col, the upper part of that range of rocks appeared almost to touch the Dent d'Erin, but as we descended an enormous valley opened between them, and a system of séraques disclosed itself at the head of this valley, of such magnitude and grandeur as to recall to us those of the Géant and the Taconnay. It turned out that the lower arm of the Zmutt Glacier (to which the rocks of the Stöckhi were to give us access) took its origin beneath the very base of the Dent d'Erin, and lay embosomed in a vast hollow between that peak and the upper arm of the glacier on which we stood. The crags that overhang the lower and support the higher branch of the glacier form an amphitheatre of nearly a thousand feet in height.

Arrived upon the Stöckhi, we paused a moment to enjoy the view. The range of Monte Rosa lay in front, more than half hidden by the clouds; the Findelen Glacier alone came down out of the mist, like a huge serpent creeping towards the fertile valley. The Riffelberg Inn was very conspicuous, perched on the heights above Zermatt. Beneath the "long low ridge" of the northern side of the Col, was one unbroken range of magnificent precipices, forming a jealous and hopeless barrier to the glacier of Zmutt. Nearly opposite the Stöckhi, this wall of rock recedes, forming a deep and wild amphitheatre, the nursery of the tributary glacier of the Schönbühl, which descends from beneath the very summit of the Dent Blanche. Nearly down to its lower extremity the glacier of Zmutt is still guarded by the same long line of tremendous precipices,— broken, however, by no less than three glacier-basins of immense size, the Hochwang, the Arbe, and the Distel,— each contributing its quota to the glacier of Zmutt. On the Hochwang I counted a number of dirt-bands, beginning at the foot of an ice-fall, and, like those of the Ferpêcle, so close to one another as to make it difficult to connect the intervals between them with the annual rate of motion of the glacier. It increases the difficulty, in this case, that the Hochwang is a very steep glacier.

A rapid descent over rocks covered with loose bits of broken stone, lasting about a quarter of an hour, brought us to the foot of the Stöckhi and to the level of the lower arm of the Zmutt Glacier. We halted for a few minutes to make some lemonade, and then started down the glacier, which was here free from new snow and not greatly crevassed. We left the Stöckhi about a quarter to one o'clock, and for some distance kept close to the base of the rock. On reaching the end of the ridge, however, we found the glacier much crevassed. The lateral pressure is in some degree removed, and, as might be expected, the crevasses begin to fall away to the left. Cachat took to the moraine, which I detest; but I felt certain that by striking towards the middle of the glacier I should come to the narrow ends of the crevasses, and probably be able to cut them nearly all at once. It was as I expected, and I found no difficulty in passing them all. I came to one very remarkable spot. There was a ridge of ice before me stretching half across the glacier; on climbing it I found beneath me, not so much a crevasse as a deep trench or valley in the ice, at least eighty feet deep, the lower side not being half so high as the upper, and the general level of the glacier appearing to undergo a corresponding alteration, I could not tell why.

For more than an hour, as we descended the long glacier of Zmutt, the rain was falling as fast as it could in the basin of the Distel Glacier on our left. The storm never seemed to move, but over that amphitheatre hung one black solid mass of cloud, out of which the rain came down in a cone. It looked just like a great shower-bath. There was a most brilliant rainbow, in which we saw every one of the colours distinctly shown behind the rain and in front of the glacier and rock. On our right the avalanches were falling constantly from the precipitous curtain joining the Dent d'Erin and the Matterhorn.

The glacier of Zmutt is very much compressed, and many of its tributaries have medial moraines of their own. In consequence of this circumstance, they are all driven so close together at the extremity of the glacier as nearly to touch one another. Seen from a little distance the whole surface appears covered with moraines, and the Zmutt may fairly claim to be considered the dirtiest glacier in Switzerland. The moraine of the Stöckhi is conspicuous not only for its size, but for the deep red which is the prevailing colour of the stones which it brings down. It preserves its characteristic aspect to the very end of the glacier.

The Hörnli Glacier is a conspicuous object on the right, descending from the northern face of the

Matterhorn. It is not safe to quit the glacier of Zmutt till the Hörnli is left well behind, as it is very prolific in avalanches; so that we had to get nearly to the bottom of the glacier of Zmutt before we could leave it and take to the mountain side. I had let my companions go on ahead, and was leaning on my stick, trying to take in the grand scenery around me, when my ear was struck by a curious sound. I listened, and after a few minutes heard again distinctly the peculiar creaking sound you get when you squeeze ice in a Bramah's press. It was the ice of the glacier straining under the operation of Nature's great press, as it was urged relentlessly through its narrowing channel.

We left the glacier at half-past two, after traversing a pre-eminently disagreeable bit of moraine-bestrewed glacier; and climbing a grassy knoll beneath the Schwarzsee, soon found a little path leading to the chalets of Zmutt, and thence to Zermatt. A more beautiful path I have scarcely ever seen, even amongst the Alps, and I counsel visitors to Zermatt to add a trip to the Zmutt Glacier, if possible, to the number of their excursions. The mountain side is well clothed with masses of splendid dark firs, mixed with larches, dressed, when we saw them, in autumn's rich and russet tints. Every here and there the woods give way to patches of pasture land, of more than common fertility. There is a long wood-walk, which we thought all too short, beneath dark frowning crags, with lichen-clad firs and larches on either hand. It winds its way amongst moss-grown boulders and out-croppings of rock, which thrust themselves up from amidst a luxuriant growth of bilberry bushes, rhododendrons, and other Alpine shrubs. By and bye, you emerge on to steep slopes of verdant turf, watered by little rills of glacier water, whence a welcome view of Zermatt, with its bright glittering spire and comfort-promising hostelries, is obtained. Then a narrow bridge is crossed, over a roaring cataract which thunders at a great depth below, and just leaves room for a path between its channel and a set of great cliffs towering to a height of more than a thousand feet above it, and a few minutes more bring you to the pleasant meadows of Zermatt, and the long day's interesting work is over. It was just a quarter past four when we arrived, and saw the most welcome sight of all,— my wife, already safely housed in the inn, after a day of hardly less enjoyment than our own, and ready to exchange with us the pleasant stories of the day's adventures.

CHAP. X

"Right to the mountain's top he press'd,
But oh! what sobs the toil confess'd."

ASCENT OF MONTE ROSA.

SUPPOSED INACCESSIBILITY.—THE SCHLAGINTWEITS.—MESSRS. SMYTH.—TOPOGRAPHY OF MONTE ROSA.—AN OLD FRIEND.—COFFEE AND QUARRELS.—A SADDER AND A WISER MAN.—THE COMET.—THE GORNERGRAT.—THE GORNER GLACIER.—APPEARANCE OF MONTE ROSA.—ASCENT TO THE "SADDLE."—OUR FIRST HALT.—A TERRIBLE WIND.—A NARROW RIDGE.—THE HÖCHSTE SPITZE.—GRAND PANORAMA.—THE NORD END SPITZE.—HEIGHT OF THE "SADDLE."—MAGNIFICENT CREVASSES. — FATIGUING DESCENT. — A PLEASANT MEETING. — THE RIFFELBERG.

MONTE ROSA is, in point of height, the second mountain in Europe — being only two or three hundred feet lower than the great monarch of the Alps. For a long time, it even disputed the palm with its mighty rival, but the more accurate explorations and measurements of modern times have conclusively established its inferiority. It is said to derive its name from the rich hues often flung upon its ample snows by the glowing lights of ebbing day: and perhaps the enormous amphitheatre formed by the chain of which it is the principal component, with its western exposure, may be peculiarly favourable to the reflection upon its peak of the ruddy rays of sunset. Till a few years ago, its boasted inaccessibility added the fascination of mystery to the unaided and obvious attractions of the scenery. No human being had ever reached that sharp peak of mingled rock and snow, which, in some lights and from some spots, looked but a stone's throw from the spectator. The difficulties were said to be terrible, but what they were no one could tell, for no spirit had arisen hardy enough to brave the genius of the mountain in his own stronghold — and as usual, the unknown was universally accepted as the terrible. Some years ago, a great Swiss geologist, Professor Ulrich, of Berne, made a resolute attempt to master this invincible difficulty; but, assailed by storm and wind, he was compelled to halt when still a considerable distance from the top; and, though his guides went on by themselves, he was unable to quit the protection of the rock behind which he was sheltering from the tempest, and could neither confirm nor refute the pretensions they made to the honour of having stood on that summit whereon man had never stood before. Lower peaks, however, than the actual summit were gained from time to time, by one hardy climber after another; and at length, in 1851, the Schlagintweits of Berlin succeeded in reaching the actual top of Monte Rosa. The first Englishmen who accomplished the feat were the Messrs. Smyth, three well-known Alpine travellers.* The difficulties of the last few hundred feet, they described as of the most formidable character; but succeeding adventurers varied the course which they had taken, and avoided some of the worst of the dangers they had incurred.

There still remains, and ever must remain, one long ridge, or rather succession of ridges, along the very edge of which the final ascent, of some twelve or fifteen hundred feet, must be made, where no person who is not proof against giddiness and vertigo has any right to trust himself. During the whole of this

* I had always supposed that the Messrs. Smyth were the first travellers who gained the summit of Monte Rosa, until I fell in accidentally with an interesting little work, published at Aosta in 1855, entitled "Les Alpes Pennines dans un jour," by the Canon Carrel of that city, in which it is said that the Schlagintweits preceded the Messrs. Smyth by three years. M. Carrel is a well-known man of science, and I have no doubt he is correct. I commend his little book to those who are likely to visit Aosta or the neighbourhood; they will find a great deal of valuable information, nicely given, and in a small compass.

last ascent, the travellers, as seen from a neighbouring though far inferior height, are cut out in bold relief against the clear blue sky. In a score of places, not two feet on their right is an unprotected precipice of unfathomed depth; while on their left the ice falls so steeply away that, did they slip, there would be no halting-place for two or three thousand feet. But a "bad head" seems to be a rare phenomenon amongst the class of hardy and vigorous young Englishmen who flock in shoals to the districts about Monte Rosa; for since the fiction of its inviolability has been exploded, the excursion has become so common that hardly a week — sometimes hardly a day, in the height of the season — passes without an attempt (generally successful) to ascend Monte Rosa.

I knew the neighbourhood of Monte Rosa well, and might perhaps have been the first English traveller to scale that lofty peak. I was actually on my way to Zermatt, in September 1854, and was laying plans for the attempt on an early day, when I met the Messrs. Smyth, on their way down the valley of St. Nicholas, a day or two after their ascent. I felt reluctant to take, as it were, the edge off their success, by following instantly in their footsteps, and determined to postpone the expedition; and it chanced that the September of 1858 offered me the first favourable opportunity for making the attempt, by which time the ascent had become one of the familiar excursions of the place.

As you look at a good map of the mountain groups of the south of Switzerland, you see that Monte Rosa lies at the point of intersection of two great chains, each of which may lay some claim to it. The first is the great backbone dividing Switzerland from Italy, and running nearly east and west; the second, to which Monte Rosa more fairly belongs, is a rib, running nearly north and south, and ending at the valley of the Rhone, which it meets nearly at right angles. It is prolonged for a short distance on the south of the main chain, dividing the watercourses which supply the Lys and the Sesia, two of the tributaries of the Po. Our comparison to a rib, however, would electrify a physiologist, if we insisted upon his following us into details; for it throws off various little irregular "processes" on either side, one of which, called the Gornergrat, plays an important part in the topography of Monte Rosa, and enters largely into the calculations of every visitor to the neighbourhood. Certain sharp excrescences show themselves in the western section of the backbone (reckoning from Monte Rosa). The most remarkable of them is also the farthest to the west: it is the stupendous peak of the Matterhorn, rising in one bold, sharp, pyramidal obelisk no less than five thousand feet above the general level of the backbone, and closely rivalling Monte Rosa in height,—perhaps the most amazing object amongst the Alps. To the east of the Matterhorn lie several other huge peaks, of which the principal are the Breithorn and the Lyskamm, each nearly fifteen thousand feet above the level of the sea. Then the chain trends a little to the north, and away springs what we have called the rib — starting boldly with no less aspiring a summit than Monte Rosa itself. The important "process" of the Gornergrat is an offshoot of the Monte Rosa system, reaching an average height of eight or nine thousand feet, and marked by one irregular cone called the Riffelhorn. It runs nearly parallel with the line passing through the summits of the Breithorn and the Lyskamm, but is separated from them by a huge river of ice, called the Gorner Glacier, which descends from the heart of Monte Rosa itself, receives half a score of affluent ice-streams from the Lyskamm and the Breithorn, and at length descends into the head of the valley separating the rib of the Monte Rosa chain from the neighbouring rib to the west. The village of Zermatt lies in this valley, a few miles below the end of the glacier; and at a distance from Zermatt of two or three hours' walk, and at an elevation above it of about three thousand feet, is a pleasant turfy slope of the Gornergrat range, looking towards the north-west, called the " Riffelberg," on which a little hostelry has been built;—an accommodation due, if report speaks truly, to the enterprise of three of the neighbouring *curés;* who have found in it a most promising speculation. These topographical details are, it is to be feared, a little dry, but they could hardly be dispensed with, and we must congratulate ourselves if, among the mountains, they have brought us to no worse a goal than the clean and comfortable Riffelberg Inn.

Monday, the 20th September, was the day fixed upon for our expedition. I should have been glad enough to wait till a day later, for I had, within one week, ascended Mont Blanc, and crossed two of the greatest glacier passes in the Alps; but H., who accompanied me, was anxious to return to England, and could not spare another day. At the Riffelberg Inn, I was fortunate enough to meet with an old acquaintance, Ulrich Lauener, the boldest hunter of the Oberland, who had guided the Messrs. Smyth in their first ascent, and in the same year had accomplished with me the maiden ascent of the Wetterhorn. We had with us two of the best guides of Chamouni, and a young porter of the same place; and confident that where others could find their way, they and we should not fail, we had resolved to take no guides of the place, but to fight our own way up. I was, therefore, very glad of some information as to the route, quickly, clearly, and concisely given to me by Lauener. There was living proof for us, in the hotel, that the ascent might prove not free from risk, for a gentleman lay there, at that moment, in bed, in great suffering from frost-bite, to which he had exposed himself in an unsuccessful attempt to ascend, three or four days before, and all Switzerland was then talking of a like calamity which had befallen some English pedestrians, who had ascended in very inclement weather, about the end of August. We knew, however, from ample experience, that these accidents rarely occur where there has been no want of precaution, and even Balmat, who had so nearly lost his hands on Mont Blanc, a week before, entertained no fear of the consequences of undertaking the expedition.

After we had made all our arrangements, ordered

our provisions, and fixed our hour of starting, we learned that another English gentleman, staying in the house, was going to set off on the same expedition half-an-hour later than ourselves, and we soon came to an agreement to combine our forces — an arrangement profitable to both parties, for *we* could hardly expect not to make some blunders in shaping our course, which would make us lose time and add to our labour; and, on the other hand, as the snow was likely to be deep, eight would find it lighter work than three. We watched a glorious sunset; and as the daylight faded away, the great comet stole into life, above the mountains in the west.

The next morning we rose before two, and found a cup of hot coffee and a quarrel in readiness for us. The two guides of our new friend were "locals;" one of them belonging to Visp, the other to Zermatt. Our three men were *outsiders* from another district, and were about to commit the unpardonable offence of poaching on the Zermatt manor. There were half-a-dozen other Zermatt men in the house, and they and the landlord combined in an attempt to punish us for our interference with their "vested rights." I heard high words freely bandied about below, and, on going down stairs, found our François Cachat remonstrating against the provisions selected for our use. There was, indeed, good reason for his complaints — a leg of lean mutton, full of veins and gristle, a hunch of black bread, insufficient in quantity and bad in quality, were the staple articles offered us for a most laborious day. When the landlord saw me arrive on the scene, he slunk into a sort of den; but I ferreted him out, and remonstrated with him as the magnitude of the offence deserved. He had reproached our men with not making us take provisions enough. Other people, he said, spent sixty francs in fowls and wine, and etceteras of one sort or another: we had ordered what would not come up to a sixth of that amount. Then the local guides chimed in, and declared they would not start with us, to show our Chamouni men the way, unless we would take one of the Zermatt guides as well. One of the latter had actually dressed and breakfasted, in anticipation of being able to profit by our necessities. Of course, the landlord professed himself an ill-used innocent: he knew nothing of the confederacy against us, and to him it was a matter of pure indifference how much or how little we chose to take. Our friend of last evening now made his appearance, and found his recalcitrant guides refuse to stir. We expressed our regret at being the cause of any trouble or annoyance to him, and offered to separate from his party, and either go on ahead or follow an hour or two later, as he might choose; but he showed great courtesy and spirit,— would hear of nothing of the kind; declined any discussion with his guides, and offered them the simple choice of going with us or staying behind: it was a matter for them, he said, not for him. At the same time he joined in my onslaught on our host, and our united attacks soon silenced the enemy's fire. Better provender was sulkily brought out; and the guides, with equal sulkiness, prepared to "eat the leek," and follow in our train.

All this fracas, however, took some time, and it was quite three o'clock when we filed off from the hotel. We had been promised a lantern, the better to pick our way over the top of the Gornergrat range, but the landlord could not make up his mind to forego inflicting *some* annoyance, and he accordingly would not find it, and declared his further inability to furnish us with raisins, which are a great comfort in a long and hard ascent, and which had been readily forthcoming on the previous evening. It was, however, a great consolation to think of the Zermatt guide, his early breakfast, and his rueful face as he turned away from the door,—a sadder, and we trusted a wiser, man. One of our local friends still sulked in no common degree, and kept out of sight of us in the darkness. It was not for nearly three hours afterwards that he deigned to draw near, and give us the pleasure of his company. The other, a smart, brisk, merry, good-tempered fellow, recovered himself directly, and apologized for having appeared in the mess at all: he was of Visp; and he declared (whether truly or not it is impossible to say) that the Zermatt men threatened him with a sound beating if he did not join their faction. At all events, if he had been less unwilling to do so than he represented himself, he made the best atonement he could for his error, and proved himself active and intelligent, thoroughly conversant with the route, a bold iceman, a bold cragsman, and a cheerful and pleasant companion.

It was a perfect September night. The temperature was 4°·5 Centigrade (about 40° Fahrenheit), and the stars shone brightly out of a cloudless sky. The comet was now descending rapidly towards the dark outline of the Gornergrat; the magnificent constellation of Orion was in front of us, and seemed like a bright omen of success, as we groped our way across the broken turf by which we had to ascend to a gap in the ridge, where the path to the glacier begins. The omen, interpreted aright, however, betokened a not unclouded day; for some of the largest stars were surrounded by a thin veil of mist, through which their bright rays bravely fought their way, and reached us scarcely less brilliant than they were before encountering the vapour. We could scarcely see a trace of snowy mountains before us: Monte Rosa and the neighbouring summits are not visible from the Riffelberg, being hidden by the intervening range of the Gornergrat.

When we first started, the Matterhorn towered in solitary grandeur on our right, his great glaciers streaming down on every side, and lighting up the gloom of the deep valley beneath with a dim and spectral light. We turned to the left almost at once, and left him behind us; and as we rose gently on the soft turf of the Gornergrat, a huge wall of crag and snow loomed upon us through the darkness, and we distinguished the Breithorn, and to its left the Lyskamm, and, last of all, the great mountain we were about to assail, which, with a due regard to effect, was concealed from us for some time after the other peaks were full in view. The effect of that dim starlight on glacier scenery is peculiarly striking: it is impossible to form any conception of the actual or relative distances of different objects; and when we reached the gap of the Gornergrat, the great Gorner Glacier, which swept beneath our feet many hundreds of feet below us, seemed so close that a step or two ought to bring us to it. We had, however, a good hour's walk before we reached it, for it stretches out its long length for several miles at the foot of the Gornergrat range; and a little path has been cut in the mountain side, descending very gently all the way, by which you gain the glacier at no great distance from the base of Monte Rosa. This path is safer by night than by day, for it is a favourite pastime with visitors to the Gornergrat (with ladies, especially, I am told,) to roll down stones from above, which render the passage neither agreeable nor safe. The path requires some little caution in the dark, for in one or two places it passes at the top of precipitous gullies, or on ledges in smooth slabs of rock, down which you would go much further than you liked, if you chanced to slip. It was somewhere about half-past four when we reached the ice, and climbed up the sloping bank which forms the edge of the glacier. It was freezing very hard, as we found out, for it was necessary to help ourselves up the first few paces with our hands as well as our knees. Here my friend H. had the misfortune to drop his alpenstock into a crevasse, whence it could not be recovered; and one of our men was obliged, in consequence, to go without a stick the whole day long—a great addition to his labour.

After passing a few yards further on to the glacier, the ice was entirely uncrevassed; but we had to pick our way with care, to avoid stumbling into little pits of water, of which it was singularly full. They were just frozen over, and if we had wet our feet thoroughly by stepping into them, there might have been serious risk of frost-bite later in the day. It was rapidly getting lighter, however, and we were all fortunate enough to escape a wetting of any consequence. The break of day was very grand. It was later in the season than I have been accustomed to watch it on such expeditions, and the dull, dead violet, which I first noticed over the precipices of the Lyskamm, was to me a most unusual tint. It reminded me strongly of the skies in pictures and panoramas I have seen of scenes in the Arctic regions. The glacier appears but a stone's throw across, when seen from the Gornergrat, but it was quite light before we had traversed it, and a delicate rosy blush, the herald of the day, reflected from the sky above or from some cloud in the east, was flung over the long, snowy,

I sh...
...ylight, I
...pt in th...
... peak ...
Monte Rosa ...
... the ...
...ful pr...
...ied, ... the ...
... m...ding ...
... of "Aiguilles ...
... ...cends from ... three ...
... right and left, ...ding th... "h..."
...brace, while the middle portion ... ... the
very heart of the m...... itse... As we ...
face to face with Monte Rosa, on the ...tr...portion
of the Gorner Glacier, looking into the great ... ...
...sin out of which it comes forth on its l...
the valley, where the ... ...ce is ...
fade away, and to ... ...
I..., an impetuous and resistless move...
...see that the least elevated portion ... glacier
lies t...our left, and has its origin ... ...
of snow connecting the upper extre...
Gornergrat range with the mass of M...
... beneath the mountain, ...
height of perhaps ten or eleven ...

rounded summit of the Lyskamm. It was not the true daylight, however, for the great Matterhorn still slept in the dead cold white which is the hue of lofty peaks before daylight breaks.

Monte Rosa rises at the head of the Gorner Glacier in one huge hump, totally destitute of the graceful proportions of Mont Blanc. Nor is it surrounded, like the monarch of the Alps, by a forest of those needle-like peaks to which the appropriate name of " Aiguilles " has been given. The Gorner Glacier streams from it in three great arms—those on the right and left holding the " hump " in a close embrace, while the middle portion issues from the very heart of the mountain itself. As we stand face to face with Monte Rosa, on the central portion of the Gorner Glacier, looking into the great rocky basin out of which it comes forth on its long journey to the valley, where the ice-existence is destined to fade away, and to take a new and more vigorous life, as an impetuous and resistless mountain torrent, we see that the least elevated portion of the glacier lies to our left, and has its origin in the long ridge of snow connecting the upper extremity of the Gornergrat range with the mass of Monte Rosa. Close underneath the mountain, the ridge attains a height of perhaps ten or eleven thousand feet; but

Monte Rosa itself shoots forth from it, in a broken wall of nearly perpendicular rock, which can scarcely be less than two thousand feet high. Above this huge precipice is a long, sharp ridge of snow, leading up to the Nord End Spitze, the northernmost of several points which are all called by the generic name of summits. From the lower part of this snow-ridge springs another set of precipices, coming forward towards the spectator with a rapidly lowering outline. This range curves gently round from its highest to its lowest portion, bending from right to left, and then again from left to right, like the printer's mark at the beginning of a parenthesis. The other mark, to complete the parenthesis, is the right-hand boundary of the mass of Monte Rosa—a series of precipitous cliffs of rock, broken by steep curtains and rounded faces of glacier, which bind together the higher and the lower systems of crags. The parenthetical matter included between these two gigantic curves could hardly be left out without seriously damaging the general effect, for it comprehends the great central basin of Monte Rosa— the reservoir of the middle arm of the Gorner Glacier. The two parenthesis-marks form a considerable portion of a circle. The circle, however, would be one inclined at a very steep angle to a horizontal plane, for the edge of the rocky wall on either hand rises very steeply, all the way from the foot of Monte Rosa nearly to the summit. The two boundaries, right and left, converge at the bottom, and force the vast mass of glacier which descends from the central portion of Monte Rosa to pass at length down a steep but even incline through a comparatively narrow passage, its only means of escape into the valley down which the collection of glacier systems from Monte Rosa, the Lyskamm, and the Breithorn, descend towards Zermatt.

The rounded irregular basin which occupies the central portion of Monte Rosa is filled with ice from top to bottom. Three or four considerable masses of rock alone diversify the vast extent of white. These masses group themselves in a kind of dotted inner ring within the greater boundary just described, and, with the humps which form the lowest portion of either of the great boundary systems, make a very tolerable circle. Their effect upon the glacier is shown by the dirtier aspect it wears beneath them; due mainly to boulders, débris, and dust, partly rubbed off them by the movement of the glacier, partly split away by the action of alternate thaw and frost, and scattered by wind and tempest over the surface of the snow. Above them all is white and dazzling. Dome after dome of swelling snow rises from this ring of rocks nearly to the summit of the mountain, each either separated from its neighbour by a long wall of broken shattered ice-cliffs, now very generally termed "séraques," or connected with one another by a smooth curtain of unbroken snow. The upper part of the glacier system is little crevassed, and it is easy to see from below, or with more certainty from the Gornergrat, that the peculiar difficulties of Mont Blanc — the huge gulphs of crevasses and the labyrinths of broken and tumbled ice which must be passed — do not exist on Monte Rosa. On the other hand, it is equally easy to see that the ascent of the actual summit, a steep cone of mingled rock and glacier, may present most formidable difficulties of its own.

The left-hand boundary of the Gorner Glacier — the range so often named as the Gornergrat — from its highest portion, called the Hochthäligrat, where rock and glacier unite nearly at the same level, to its lower extremity, a few miles above Zermatt, contributes nothing to the glacier stream. The right-hand boundary is perhaps the grandest chain of summits in the Alps, beginning with the Lyskamm, which is joined by a short snowy ridge to Monte Rosa, and separated from it by a deep valley, filled with a majestic and much-crevassed glacier, whence both mountains rise in precipitous majesty, continuing with the inferior peaks of the Zwillinge, or Castor and Pollux, the vast and frowning mass of the Breithorn, the smaller summit of the Little Mont Cervin, and ending in the awful pinnacle of the Matterhorn. The whole of this long line of rock and snow makes constant contributions to the Gorner Glacier. How one comparatively narrow channel can receive all the huge ice-streams which pour into it, and convey their united contents to the valley below, strikes one as one of the greatest of the many marvels of the glacier world. Besides inferior glacier masses which overhang the Gorner in several places, no less than four enormous glaciers flow down from the intervals between these great peaks, or from beneath their bases, the two largest being themselves compounds, each of two distinct affluents. So great an accumulation of ice forced into so narrow a bed is probably nowhere else to be seen.

But I am forgetting the actual ascent for the wonders of the way. About half past five we came to the rocks forming the western or right-hand boundary of the central glacier system of Monte Rosa. The sun was really rising now, for the Matterhorn was just tipped with gold. Here we left the glacier and climbed for about half an hour with great ease up the rocks. They were highly polished and rounded — *moutonnés*, as it is called — by the action of the glacier at some former period, when it must have covered them; but also much broken up into separate masses, between which charming tufts of short rough Alpine grass were growing. It was getting near six o'clock when we reached a little valley of rocks, into which a tongue of glacier descended, and here we left a portion of our provisions and took first to the snows of Monte Rosa himself. The next three or four hours' ascent was to constitute the laborious part of the day's work. It is almost entirely up this right-hand side of the glacier system of Monte Rosa that the ascent of it is made. A certain hollow or gap between the actual summit on the left, and a snowy protuberance on the right, lying very nearly straight above the point we had reached, is called the "Saddle," and it is from this "Saddle" that the last and formidable climb must be begun.

To reach this "Saddle," which we gained three or four hours later, we diverged less to the right or to the left than in any other great ascent I have made. We began by scaling a slope of snow broken by rocks, of about 38°, as measured by the clinometer. In the afternoon we descended this slope in less than five minutes, but it took us a good half hour to climb it. This brought us to a fine snowy dome, surmounting one of the faces of rock I have described as forming the right-hand boundary of the glacier system. We now made a short slanting course to the right, and then, addressing ourselves straight to the next slope of snow, passed without the least difficulty through a portion of the glacier where alone I should have anticipated some embarrassment from the crevasses. We now entered one of those delusive *hollows*, which, seen from below, are always supposed to give a space of level, if not of descending, walking; but which always turn out quite otherwise. It was a relief, however, for the incline was gentle, which is more than I can say for most of Monte Rosa. Another slope was now climbed, at the top of which we passed again through a small system of crevasses, and emerged into a second seeming hollow, where we had on our left a magnificent wall of ruddy crags, hundreds of feet high, which ran by our side for many minutes, though from the Gornergrat they look like a mere speck. Then came another steep and unbroken slope, up which we were obliged to zig-zag. Each time we reached the right-hand end of our zig-zags, we were rewarded by a grand view of the great system of precipices, raising this part of Monte Rosa above the Lyskamm valley. They cannot be less than from a thousand to fifteen hundred feet in height. Arrived at the top of this slope, we found ourselves at the brink of a long, wide, and deep crevasse, so completely masked that it was not till we looked over the ridge of snow which formed its lower edge, that we had a suspicion of its existence. We had to go far to the right to turn it; and then entered upon the last and steepest of the snow-slopes, up which we zig-zagged perseveringly, against an ever increasing inclination, till all at once we found ourselves unexpectedly walking more on a level, and a few steps brought us to the long-wished-for " Saddle."

During the greater part of this ascent the cold was intense; for the last two hours the snow had been quite dry and powdery, showing that even the midday sun of the previous days, hot as it had seemed to us in the valleys, had had no power to melt it, and consequently the cold of the night had had no effect in compacting it, and had rendered no service to the climber. At every step we sank nearly to the knees, and even then hardly found secure footing. It was difficult to keep one's feet from freezing. In spite of rabbits' fur wrapped round the toes, and secured and supplemented by a coating of grease (an invaluable precaution), in spite of two pairs of stockings, it was only by dint of energetic kicking of one foot against the other, that any ghost of life was kept in them. The mountain itself had lain between us and sunlight; once, soon after nine o'clock, we had come upon the welcome beams, straggling, if I remember right, through the "Saddle" itself; and for some short time we had enjoyed the cheering rays. I remember particularly feeling some little warmth as we skirted the long and deep crevasse, but the slope became steeper, and we entered the shade it cast. The wind at the same time became stronger and keener, and we toiled up the last snow-slopes exposed to cold of no common kind. I was feeling greatly the fatigues of the last week, which my friend H. had not fully shared; he had ascended Mont Blanc two days before myself, and had had two days of comparative rest, while I was making that expedition. It is not to be wondered at, therefore, that I had been pounding on for some time in a state of mind and body by no means to be envied. My limbs tottered, my heart beat violently, my eyes shut against my will, and nothing but a stern application of a maxim of Balmat's, "Les pantalons blancs ne reculent jamais," (I wore a pair of white flannel cricketing trousers,) carried me on. It was only objects of powerful interest that roused me. For instance, on meeting the sunlight it had been proposed to take a glass of wine, and that had stirred me to unwonted life. I drank freely of a vile compound of bad marsala, cognac, and water, dignified by the pretentious name of "old sherry" (save the mark!). The great crevasse was exquisitely bedecked with icicles, and its grim depth of beautiful horrors sufficed to rouse me again from my trance. Within a few yards of the "Saddle" we passed the end of a wild abyss of crevasse, evidently part of a "bergschrund," at the foot of the far steeper slope above, into which the most wearied or incurious passer-by could hardly look without interest or excitement.

On the "Saddle" itself, however, apathy was out of the question. A few rocks jutted up on either hand, and below them almost a sheer precipice of ice and snow fell away to an enormous glacier basin on the other side, whose existence we had not so much as conjectured before, but which takes its origin in the precipices beneath the summit, or Höchste Spitze, itself, and is bounded by the ridge connecting Monte Rosa with the Lyskamm. That ridge we had imagined to be close to the "Saddle;" but now, for the first time, we saw that it sweeps away from beneath the Höchste Spitze, and lies far back from the ridge on which we stood. I have rarely gazed down so very precipitous a wall of rock and ice and snow as that on which we were now perched. To our right was a little hump of snow; but the point of interest was on our left, for there lay a long, narrow ridge of ice, crowned with outcropping rocks, and rising very sharply from our feet. This was the beginning of the famous cone of Monte Rosa himself; and the narrow portal through which we gazed upon the depths of the glacier below was the spot now so well known to Alpine wanderers as the "Saddle."

We now called a halt, the first of any consequence we had made since starting. We had breakfasted at two, and it was now nearly ten o'clock, and we all felt that food was a necessity. We descended a few feet on the further side of the "Saddle," to some straggling rocks. It was ludicrous enough to see us, all blue in the face with cold, and kicking our feet against the rocks as hard as we could, to revive them. There was sunlight, but it was dimmed by having to pierce some white clouds, so that it caused us little warmth, and the wind was as fearful as any I ever encountered. It is difficult for any one who has had no experience of them to form a conception of what these mountain winds are on elevated summits. They are armed with a dry, scorching, penetrating cold, against which no clothing is proof, and they facilitate frost-bite more than any other accident of weather. Balmat had nearly lost his hands on Mont Blanc, a week before, and I was in real anxiety about him, especially as his feet also were very much benumbed. Mine were very cold, but not quite so senseless as his. I believe all of us would have been in danger if we had had to submit to that wind for many minutes. Still, eating and drinking were absolutely necessary, though we performed them as speedily as we could — so hurriedly that, I regret to say, I left a valuable many-bladed knife — a very old friend — behind me on the rocks. We had brought some champagne with us—an inestimable resource in the mountains — and it put new life and vigour into us all; and in a very few minutes we had resumed our journey. The knapsacks were left behind at the " Saddle," and an apparatus for boiling water, as a means of measuring heights, I was reluctantly obliged to leave also, for

I felt that I had no right to endanger myself or others by staying to use it in such a climate.

The Höchste Spitze, for which we were bound, was not visible at first, being concealed by the ridge we had now to climb; but shortly after we started, a slight bend in the direction of the ridge revealed it towering still nearly a thousand feet above us. I confess I had very little hope of being able to reach it, in the face of the awful blast which was shrieking and roaring about us; but, by a fortunate accident, we had not been ten minutes on our way when it began to fall, and before long it was almost a calm. Sometimes, the steep slope we had to mount is all hard ice; then every step must be cut with the hatchet, and the process is long and most fatiguing. Happily for us, the very edge of the ridge was snow, and we were able to dispense almost entirely with step-cutting. In many places, at a couple of feet to our left, all was hard as ice and smooth as glass. To our right was a few inches' width of snow, and then a rocky precipice. The precipice was sometimes absolutely perpendicular, and of course quite bare of snow, and for scores of feet marked by nothing to break the sheer descent; sometimes merely so steep as to be the next thing to perpendicular. Nowhere, however, could we see more than a few dozen feet down the wall of rock: and then the next object was the glacier basin, a good thousand feet beneath!

We toiled slowly up the snow, for the ridge was very steep (I measured it in descending, and found the angle 36°), and there was no room to zig-zag. At length the snow ended, and we took to a narrow ledge of rocks. The description usually given is literally true. It was in no place more than three feet wide; in many, not a third of that width. On the right is a precipice; on the left a bank of snow, so steep as to be just as bad. This sounds awful enough; but I must say that to me the passage seemed, as we found it, destitute alike of danger and difficulty. The rocks are solid, not friable and treacherous as on the Wetterhorn; there is good hand-hold and foot-hold, and a slip seemed to me all but impossible. I can conceive that, when covered with ice, as they often are, they may require the utmost caution; but we had the singular good fortune to find our path thickly paved with snow, or metalled with the solid rock. I can give no better idea of my own feeling of security than by the following fact. In spite of fingerless gloves, well lined with foxes' fur, my hands were numbed and senseless; and, in order to warm them, I stuck first one, and then the other, into the waistband of my trousers, and actually walked nearly all the way along this terrible ridge with only one hand disengaged. I remember well one place where the ridge was narrowest. There were two large blocks of stone, three or four feet apart. Between them was a little hollow, filled with snow, and in the snow I saw the footprints of my predecessors, in the hollow. It never occurred to me to go down and up again, and I jumped from one block to the other, as a matter of course.

From the top of the first snow-slope we saw exactly what lay before us — a short clambering descent, a narrow level ridge of snow, then a second ridge, shorter, but very much steeper than the first, and above that another narrow ridge of rocks. Of course, it was the same sort of work again; but if that short connecting ridge were ice instead of snow, it would be the worst place of all to cross, and I am inclined to think I should prefer to sit astride and work myself along in that position. These horizontal ridges are far more trying to walk along than those which have a steep inclination, and they are always narrower. This, being of snow and not of ice, offered no difficulty, and the last ridge was quickly attacked. It proved in equally good condition with the first, and led us to a steep climb over the rocks, ending in a couple of little chimneys, one after the other. Near the top of the second, a rock had fallen in, and half filled it up, so that passing it was like climbing round a projecting coping. However, hands and knees will do a good deal, and so far on our day's journey this was not likely to stop us. Being tired, I had gone last, not to hinder any one else, and on poking my head out of the top of the second chimney, I found, to my great surprise, "no more worlds to conquer," nothing but blue sky above me, my companions already seated about on one ledge or another — and I was on the top of Monte Rosa.

It is literally true that on the summit of Monte Rosa there is not room for two persons to stand at a time; but there is a mass of jumbled rocks about the summit, on which we all found space to stand, and even to move about. On every side abrupt precipices fall away from the Höchste Spitze. The most abrupt are on the north-west, or Gornergrat side, and here I, being securely tied by a rope, descended three or four feet, and scraping away the snow, built up a little construction of stones, within which I placed a self-registering thermometer, and covered it again, to the depth of two or three feet, with snow. I was not able to go there again, as I had hoped to do, in 1859, and I do not suppose I shall now ever learn to what point it has descended.

The panoramic view from Monte Rosa is one of almost unrivalled interest. I cannot compare it with that of Mont Blanc, for twice has the weather been against me, and I do not yet know what is to be seen from that, the only peak in Europe loftier than Monte Rosa; but my friend H., who had had a glorious view ten days before from Mont Blanc, declared that it was quite eclipsed by what we now beheld. There were, alas! multitudes of clouds, but they did not form a solid bank of impenetrable obscurity, as when I stood that day week, almost at the same hour, on the summit of Mont Blanc. The clouds, as usual, lay thickest on the Italian side; but between them we saw plainly the Lago Maggiore, the plains of Italy, and the distant Apennines. The Sesia springs from a huge glacier situated almost at our feet; but the Sesia's tide was yet uncrimsoned, and the heavy clouds that floated below us were charged with fertility, not with desolation. I little thought, as I gazed upon the rich and peaceful scene—so grateful a contrast to the eternal snow and lifeless rocks which encompassed us — what deeper and more tragic interests would shortly gather round that fated land, or how soon amidst those fruitful plains would

> . . "some stream obscure, some uncouth name,
> By deeds of blood be lifted into fame."

Least of all, was there anything to suggest to us that aught was threatening in the west, for there the whole range of Mont Blanc stood out sharp and clear against the blue sky. The great "Calotte" of the Alpine monarch, the Mur de la Côte, the Col du Géant, the Grandes Jorasses, the Aiguille Verte, were as distinctly visible as on a map. We saw them nearly over the ridge of the Lyskamm. A vast mountain stood out much nearer to us, in majestic proportions. It was the Grand Combin; behind which was displayed the rugged outline of the Vélan, though in diminished size. Nearly in a line with these, but of course much nearer to us, rose the sharpest and sublimest of the peaks of Europe — the stupendous Matterhorn — a narrow pyramid of rock, scarcely flecked with snow, and literally looking higher from where we stood than it did from the valley of Zermatt, nearly eleven thousand feet below. No words can convey the grandeur of the range of peaks of which the Matterhorn now formed the intermediate point — the

Lyskamm, the Zwillinge, the Breithorn, the Little Mont Cervin, leading up to him along a huge rampart of rock and glacier streaming with a score of vast ice-rivers pouring down towards the great central flood of the Gorner; the chain continuing with the Gabelhörner, the Rothhorn, the Weisshorn, and the Bruneckhorn, over which were seen a multitude of inferior summits. The Dent d'Erin, which I had seen two days before from the Col d'Erin, to the right of the Matterhorn, and rivalling it in sublimity, now lay to the left of that peak, and was dwarfed into comparatively insignificant dimensions. To the north and north-west the eye ranged over a troubled sea of peaks, in which the great summits of the Oberland were of course conspicuous; the Jungfrau standing up in one sharp, well-defined pyramid, followed by the long ridge of the Eigher, after which came the pointed peak of the Finsteraarhorn. Rather nearer, and very prominent, were the twin summits of the Engelhörner, and nearer still the huge rocky masses of the Aletschhorn, with the great glacier of the Aletsch streaming round its base. Far, far away, beyond all these nearer ranges, are the snowy peaks of the Grisons; and further still in the east and south-east even the distant groups of the Ortler Spitze, and the Bernina; so that even the two score leagues that roll between us and the remote Tyrol, are as nothing to the eyes that gaze on them from this commanding station.

Perhaps, after all, some of the sublimest objects are the nearer ones. North of us rises a fearful peak at no great distance, and scarce two hundred feet lower than our own; but connected with the Höchste Spitze by a ridge so steep that we could not see the portions close to us. This is the Nord End Spitze, which from many a point of view appears the true summit, and which from what we saw I believe to be far more difficult of access than Monte Rosa itself. Beneath it, to the right, so near that one would fancy it possible to throw a stone upon it, lies Macugnaga, at least two miles of absolute depth below. The highest part of the famous Weiss Thor passage, and the fearful precipices down which a passage may be won from Zermatt to Macugnaga, were excellently seen. The sharp outline of the Nord End Spitze forbade us to follow the whole of the pass, from the head of the Hochthäligrat ridge to the commencement of the descent.

It is often reckoned three hours' work to reach the summit of Monte Rosa from the "Saddle." In our case they had dwindled into one. It was barely eleven when we gained the top, and, despite the cold, we managed to stay there three quarters of an hour, when, being all chilled to the bones, we thought it as well to descend. I remember well how my teeth chattered, and all the bones in my body seemed to be playing rough music against one another. The descent required some caution and all one's eyesight, but by a quarter past twelve we were all seated once more upon the "Saddle," where happily the wind was now moderate, and I was able to boil some water. The "Saddle" I make by this test to be about 6,160 feet above the Riffelberg. Oddly enough, I have not been able to find any reliable measurement of the Riffelberg, but I made boiling-water observations at 2 A.M. and at 5 P.M. on this day; and, comparing both of them with the simultaneous barometric readings at Geneva and at the St. Bernard, I get a mean from the four results of 8368 feet. If this be correct, the height of the "Saddle" is about 14,500 feet above the level of the sea. But I strongly suspect the results are a little too high both for the Riffelberg and for the "Saddle."

We started down again about one o'clock. The snow was excessively fatiguing. It was quite powdery; and the sun, which was now oppressively hot, seemed to have no power to melt it. In fact, whenever I took any up in my hand, I found it required some length of exposure to the heat of the hand before it could be squeezed into a snowball. I was by this time getting very tired; but I could not help turning aside to look at the grand crevasses we passed every now and then. One of them extended for hundreds of yards, with a breadth varying from fifty to a hundred feet: it showed, in long lines of horizontal stratification, the beds of snow of many a different year, and vast icicles hung from the upper edge to a depth of many feet. In another place, a great cliff of glacier, separating a lower from an upper dome, overhung the perpendicular by many degrees, and displayed along its face no less than fifteen beds of snow, belonging to as many successive years. By and by I was wholly unable to stand the pace of my fresher companions, and sent them on ahead, while Balmat and I followed at our leisure. I was glad of the gentler pace on another account, as it allowed me to look at many things for which I had not time before. The grandeur of some of the rock precipices on our left struck me very much, and in one place it was enhanced by the débris of a magnificent "séraque," which had tumbled over since we had passed by in the morning. Presently we came upon three great crevasses, presented endways to us, and running parallel to one another in the direction of the Matterhorn. We fought our way through the deep snow to gaze into them, and found two of them to be actual valleys in the ice, not less than 100 feet wide and 200 feet deep, one side overhanging the base by many feet, and with several successive rows of icicles depending from the softer snow at the top.

The sun beat down on to these exposed slopes with uncommon force, and there was not a breath of air to take off from the effect of the burning heat reflected from the snow. I experienced an exhaustion such as I have rarely felt. The snow-slopes had seemed long enough in mounting, but now I fancied them actually longer, and several times I was obliged to fling myself on my back on the snow, and to lie there some minutes before I could proceed. The great curtain above the last rocks appeared an *ignis fatuus;* the nearer we approached, the farther it receded. However, even it was reached at last, and we had a fine view of the rocks below, on either side, composing the barrier of the aperture through which the central glacier descends. Those on the right were gneiss, those on the left granite. At the bottom of this slope we entered on the little defile conducting from the glacier to the rocks; and just before reaching it I noticed a curious phenomenon which had escaped me in the morning. Several lines of moraine, at a few feet from one another, were ranged side by side with the nicest parallelism. We turned aside to examine them, and found they had all come from some precipices above, whence they had tumbled on to the glacier, and had been brought down in regular lines without any lateral displacement.

There is a great difference, after all, between going up hill and going down hill, and, despite my deadly fatigue, I reached the rocks, where H. was waiting for me, by half-past two, and after a short quarter of an hour's rest and a drink of lemonade manufactured on the spot, was ready to continue my homeward route. By the time we reached the Gorner Glacier, my exhaustion had so entirely disappeared that we prolonged our walk very materially, by continuing on the glacier for several miles, and turning aside hither and thither in all directions to examine the numerous objects of interest it presented. A steep climb of twenty minutes up the side of the Gornergrat, brought us suddenly upon my wife, sketching and wondering where we could have gone; for although she had traced us from eight in the morning, she had lost sight of us when we descended the rocks above the Gorner Glacier, and could never distinguish us again on its broad and trackless surface. A short and pleasant half-hour's walk and talk brought us all safely to the Riffelberg, where we were quietly settled by five o'clock, after a day of (to me) uncommon fatigue, but also of unusual interest.

I was very glad, the next morning, that we had not taken the day's rest I had so much wished for. The clouds hung heavy on Monte Rosa, it was snowing on many of the neighbouring peaks, and the wind was fearful. As we sat on the Gornergrat, my wife completing her sketches, and I at her side jotting down the outlines from which this sketch has been filled up, I heard it raging furiously, howling and screeching far above my head in the clear open sky, where there was nothing to provoke its fury. Against such a blast we should have had no chance of success, and should have been happy enough if we had met with no accident.

THE END.

LONDON
PRINTED BY SPOTTISWOODE AND CO.
NEW-STREET SQUARE

TRAVELLERS' EDITION OF PEAKS & PASSES.

Just published, in 16mo. price 5s. 6d. half-bound,

PEAKS, PASSES, AND GLACIERS

A SERIES OF

EXCURSIONS BY MEMBERS OF THE ALPINE CLUB.

Edited by JOHN BALL, M.R.I.A., F.L.S., President.

Travellers' Edition (being the Fifth), comprising all the Mountain Expeditions and the Maps, printed in a condensed form adapted for the Traveller's knapsack or pocket.

IT has been frequently suggested by members of the Alpine Club and other Alpine travellers, that an edition of "Peaks, Passes, and Glaciers," in a portable form suitable for carrying in the knapsack, without the coloured plates, but with the maps, would be a convenient travelling manual for explorers in the higher regions of the Alps. The present edition has therefore been prepared for this purpose, and will, it is hoped, be found an acceptable publication by the general reader, who may be glad to have this series of narratives of adventurous expeditions among the Swiss mountains brought within his reach at a more moderate price, although without the attraction of the coloured views.

The new tariff of the Chamounix Guides is included in the volume, and will doubtless be found a useful assistance by those who carry the volume with them in their excursions.

Now ready, in fcp. 8vo. with Woodcuts and Map, price 4s. 6d.

THE OLD GLACIERS OF NORTH WALES AND SWITZERLAND.

By A. C. RAMSAY, F.R.S. and G.S., Local Director of the Geological Survey of Great Britain, and Professor of Geology in the Government School of Mines. Revised and reprinted from *Peaks, Passes, and Glaciers,* and forming a Guide to the Geologist in North Wales.

"MR. RAMSAY has given us in this little volume a reprint of his contribution to *Peaks, Passes, and Glaciers,* — thus reproducing in a very portable form pages which will constitute an invaluable companion to the tourist in North Wales, where the other experiences of the Alpine Club would not be necessary to his knapsack...... The most unlearned tourist may take Mr. Ramsay's work and follow the tracks which he points out. For this book is not interesting alone to the scientific reader; it avoids as much as possible the technical vocabulary of the geologist and mineralogist, and renders its descriptions with a hearty and fluent freshness which only a genuine love of nature could inspire. And there are few travellers so unimaginative, so obdurate to the spell which the most poetic of mountains throws, as not to be set a-thinking more or less in a speculative way by Mr. Ramsay's observations." JOHN BULL.

London: LONGMAN, GREEN, and CO. Paternoster Row.

THE FOURTH EDITION.

Just published, in 1 vol. square crown 8vo. with numerous Maps,
coloured Illustrations, and Woodcuts, price 21s. cloth,

PEAKS, PASSES, AND GLACIERS

A SERIES OF EXCURSIONS
BY MEMBERS OF THE ALPINE CLUB.

EDITED BY JOHN BALL, M.R.I.A. F.L.S.
President of the Alpine Club.

THE public favour, which has been extended towards the present volume in a degree unhoped for by the editor and his fellow-contributors, has called for the preparation of a fourth edition within less than six months of its first appearance. These successive opportunities have been made use of to introduce a few needful corrections in the text and the accompanying maps, and to add to the third edition a translation of the new regulations established for the guides at *Chamouni*. A notice of some Excursions made by Members of the Alpine Club during the summer of 1859 is given in the Preface. The Eight Swiss Maps, accompanied by a Table of the Heights of Mountains, may be had separately, price 3s. 6d. A list of the Illustrations is subjoined:—

Maps.
1. The Mont Blanc Range
2. The Mountains and Glaciers of Bagnes
3. The Glacier of Zinal, and the adjoining Mountains
4. The Range of Monte Rosa
5. The Saas Grat and the Fletsch-horn
6. The Glaciers of the Oberland
7. The Bernese Alps from the Oldenhorn to the Wildstrubel
8. The Alps of Glarus and part of the neighbouring Cantons
9. Map illustrative of the Ancient Glaciers of Part of Caernarvonshire

Chromo-lithographs.
1. The Finster Aar Horn, from the South-east
2. Mont Blanc and the Glacier du Géant from the Jardin
3. Glacier of Corbassière
4. View of the Trift Pass, from the Görnergrat
5. Ascent of the Schwärze Glacier
6. The Dom, from the Æggisch-Horn
7. View from the Châlet de Villard
8. Martinsloch and the Segnes Pass, from the South-east

Woodcuts.
1. Ice Pinnacles on the Glacier of Lechaud
2. Capucin Rock
3. Chain of Mont Blanc, from the Croix de Feuillette
4. The Graffeneire, from the Glacier of Corbassière
5. Peak of Lo Besso, Glacier of Zinal
6. View from Luc in the Einfisch Thal
7. Ice Pinnacles of the Schwärze Glacier
8.   ditto   ditto
9. The Schreckhorn, from the Upper Glacier of Grindelwald
10. Plan of the Bristenstock
11. Diagram of Roches Moutonnées by the Gorge of the Aar
12. Glacier of the Aar, filling the Hollow beyond the Kirchet
13. The Plain above the Kirchet as a Lake, with Icebergs
14. Pass of Llanberis, from the bank above Llyn Peris
15. Bloc Perché, near Derlwyn, Pass of Llanberis

Peaks, Passes, and Glaciers—continued.

Woodcuts—*continued.*

16. Roche Moutonnée with Blocs Perchés, Pass of Llanberis
17. Roche Moutonnée and Bloc Perché, near Pass of Llanberis
18. Moraines and Roches Moutonnées at the mouth of Cwm Glas
19. Roches Moutonnées, Blocs Perchés, and Moraine-mound by Llyn Llydaw
20. Section of the Pass of Llanberis
21. Cwm Graianog
22. Section across the Moraines of Llyn Idwal
23. Maen-Bras, west of Snowdon
24. An Episode in the history of the Pass of Llanberis

OPINIONS OF THE PRESS.

"*PEAKS, Passes, and Glaciers* is one of the most interesting books of continental travel that have appeared for years; and the fact of its having reached a fifth edition within the twelve-month incontestably proves its popularity with the reading and travelling public. Its information is all of the most authentic kind, being given by those who have distinguished themselves for their skill in exploring the mountainous regions of which it treats. It has been frequently suggested by members of the Alpine Club, and other Alpine travellers, that an edition in a portable form suitable for carrying in the knapsack or pocket, without the coloured plates, but with the maps, would be a convenient travelling manual for explorers in the higher regions of the Alps. Hence the present cheap and portable edition. There is something very captivating in these sketches of climbing feats and exploring exploits. The perils the travellers surmount, the wonders they achieve, and the sublimity and beauty of the grand scenes of nature outspread before them, blend the fascination of romance with the details of reality. The courage and nerve requisite for such attempts bear testimony to the well-known characteristics of the English race. This little book is particularly appropriate at the present time when so many are setting out on their tours; while to readers at home it will impart some of the enthusiasm and love of adventure which animate its writers." SUN.

"THE aim and end of the Alpine Club is a noble one. By its publications it enables different individuals among its members, by the simple and faithful account of their mountaineering experiences, to combine a record whose testimony will be of especial value to science, besides provoking in our youth a noble emulation, and giving them a taste for the higher kinds of relaxation. Any member, however humble, who is satisfied, without theorising, to put down what he sees with his eyes, and what he has gone through and done, contributes to the general result; and the general result is a knowledge which is its own reward, in the elevation of character it confers on those who ponder on the marvels of God's creation, and familiarise themselves with those phenomena which appear to the eye alike of the poet and the philosopher, the Shekinah of our modern world, the visible manifestation of the presence of the Almighty."
BLACKWOOD'S MAGAZINE.

"THIS collection of narratives is of the highest interest. Independently of the personal interest of many of the adventures, the excursions show how much has been left of the actual geography of the Alpine ranges, even in their best known portions, to be filled up and ascertained by English volunteers who go there for their annual holiday. Mont Blanc itself is not even yet thoroughly explored; but the members of the Alpine Club have contributed to correct its map, and point out where they hope to complete it still further. The papers are written for the most part by close and trained observers, keenly alive to all the strange experiences and possible surprises of the ice-world, and able to record them with truthfulness and force. Many of the writers are known as well-trained Alpine explorers, and some by published accounts of scientific and personal interest. A quiet simplicity runs through most of these narratives of remarkable daring, which adds greatly to the pleasure of reading them."
GUARDIAN.

London: LONGMAN, GREEN, and CO. Paternoster Row.

www.ingramcontent.com/pod-product-compliance
Lightning Source LLC
Chambersburg PA
CBHW031415230426
43668CB00007B/313